WINSTON CHURCHILL

IN THE MIRROR

RENÉ KRAUS *has also written*

OLD MASTER: *The Life of Jan Christian Smuts*

"The latest book on the famous Boer statesman is a full
length biographical work...which is an extremely able
analysis of the man who has most influenced the destinies
of South Africa in recent decades."
—*New York Times Book Review*

"Any life story of Smuts must include the history and problems of South Africa for the better part of a century, as
something more than a background for the personal rec-
ord. Kraus gives these succinctly, clearly and often color-
fully." —*Oakland Tribune*

"OLD MASTER is a very readable, timely and important
book. . . . It is also scholarly and sincere, and extremely
relevant to problems that will dominate the near future."
—*Chicago Sun Book Week*

Published by E. P. DUTTON & COMPANY, *Inc.*

Again he makes little journeys on the Thames, the happy husband with
the woman he loves.   (*British Official Photo*)

Winston Churchill
in the mirror

HIS LIFE IN PICTURES AND STORY

By

RENÉ KRAUS

E. P. DUTTON & COMPANY, INC.

New York, 1944

A WARTIME BOOK

S. A. JACOBS, THE GOLDEN EAGLE PRESS
MOUNT VERNON, N. Y.

This book is inscribed

to

MR. JOHN BULL

CONTENTS

Part One

STORMY PETREL

"Happy Randy"
(*Strand*)

THEY met in Cowes, on a mid-August evening in 1873: Lord Randolph Spencer Churchill, cadet of His Grace, the Duke of Marlborough, and hence penniless, and Miss Jennie Jerome, daughter of Mr. Leonard Jerome, of Madison Square, Manhattan. H. M. S. *Ariadne* lay at anchor. In honor of the Czarevitch and his exalted consort there was a ball on board.

They danced the quadrille, lancers, and minuet. Lord Randolph, in more than one way a complex young man, was a poor dancer into the bargain. It was less fatiguing to walk with him on deck, and together to watch the cool, silver moon. When their brief moonlight promenade ended, the young lord accompanied the young lady ceremoniously back to her mother. A low bow. A formal curtsy. Lord Randolph joined his friend, Colonel Edgecomb, and remarked casually: "See those two girls standing with their mother? The dark one I will make my wife!"

Miss Jennie Jerome was by no means as sudden in her decision. It took her all of three days to answer, with a slight nod, his question whether she loved him enough to marry him, and with two words: "I do!"

11

Lady
Randolph
Churchill
(*Alice Hughes*)

BOTH fathers were displeased. His Grace, the Duke, was against rapture and infatuation, rather undignified feelings. Mr. Jerome, the Wall Street tycoon, had no use for an impecunious second son of a duke. On her father's command, Jennie was shipped back to Paris. Now the Germans had left, the ladies could again stay in the only city one could possibly live in. Lord Randolph, for his part, was needed at home, to stand for Woodstock, the family constituency, which was in danger of falling to an uncle with suspicious Liberal inclinations, unless the legitimate heir to the borough contested it. Randolph despised politics, and would save the family seat only on condition that His Grace would consent to his marriage.

The Duke betook himself to Paris. He was so charmed with his prospective daughter-in-law that he himself pressed for an early wedding.

On the fifteenth of April, 1874, the wedding was performed at the British Embassy in Paris. Seven months later, on the third of December, 1874, *The Times* of London printed among its birth notices:

"On the 30th November, at Blenheim Palace, the Lady Randolph Churchill, prematurely, of a son."

From the very day of his birth, Winston was in a hurry.

12

Churchill
The boy

SOON after his second birthday, on December 11, 1876, the baby Winston, comfortably installed on a back seat of a stately victoria, entered Dublin in the cortège of the newly appointed Viceroy, his ducal grandfather. His father had become private secretary (unpaid) to His Grace. Strangely, in the atmosphere of the Old Court in Dublin, Randolph developed a taste for his old pet aversion — politics. He fell in with the "bhoys," the witty, bibulous, irascible Irish frondeurs.

Yet he remained faithful to sport and play of conservative society, to whom John Bull's other island was not a country of smoldering dissatisfaction, but the horseman's paradise. Both lightweights, the young Churchills rode their hunters recklessly. Lady Randolph admitted that she "begged, borrowed, or stole" any horse she could lay hands on.

Riding, shooting, a bit of politicking, endless rounds of social functions, completely absorbed the stylish young pair. As in many great English families in Victorian days, the little boy was rather neglected.

13

He was a strong-willed, high-strung boy. When his only confidante, his nurse, was to be replaced by a governess, he hid away in the woods. They caught him, and brought him home. The governess proved even stiffer and more rigid than Winnie had feared. Yet she did not infringe upon his dream world. He was allowed to play with his magic lantern, his real steam engine, and his two thousand lead soldiers, wearing the uniforms of all British regiments.

Family group

WHEN he was transferred to St. James' School, Ascot, even those toys were taken away. He crammed Latin into his head. "Oh, mensa," taught the schoolmaster. "You use the vocative when you address the table," he explained. "But I never speak to a table!" Winston told him.

Winston was frightfully lonesome in his school. The beautiful mother was far away. "She shone for me like the evening star," he recollected many years later. "I loved her dearly — but at a distance."

His father kept aloof, too. Lord Randolph became hopelessly involved in unorthodox politics. Not until the little boy, due to his harsh treatment in the archaic boarding school, fell seriously ill was he delivered by his parents. Now he enjoyed a short spell at home. Sometimes his father — the most handsome and admirable man on earth — sat with him. But they used to sit together in silence.

14

Father
and son

The Right
Honorable
Lord Randolph
Churchill

LORD RANDOLPH made a meteoric career — and crashed. He had become Chancellor of the Exchequer and Leader of the House with the certain expectation of succeeding to the Premiership. But after less than a year in Great Britain's second highest office, he resigned over a petty issue. Was it querulousness and petulance? Or had the flames of his rapidly consumed young life already burned down so low? Did he feel that he was under the shadow of death? Scooping even the Queen, *The Times* of December 23, 1886, announced his incomprehensible, rash decision.

MORE than a year later, when "Grandolph's" pride and fall were still the dominant topic around English dinner tables, Winston entered Harrow. He started at the bottom of the whole school, but after this poor beginning his headmaster, Dr. Welldon, was soon attracted by Winston's interest in history and by his literary gifts.

Lord Randolph, no longer "Happy Randy," mellowed. Sometimes he deigned his boys — John, eight years Winston's junior, had arrived — a serious talk.

Vacation was now a good time, even in a poverty-menaced home. Naturally, as it were, Winston assumed the supreme command of the many children of the family, the in-laws and relatives. At first they approached Master Winston reluctantly. All the nurseries in the neighborhood used to talk about him in hushed whispers. Although a brilliant child of destiny, he certainly was an *enfant terrible*. But everyone loved him. The other infants were moving in his wake. They played with the dregs of his toys, and read his discarded picture books. When Master Winston, at long last, decided to bequeath his puppet theater to his cousin and favorite friend, Shane Leslie, the latter received a dazzling but battered inheritance.

Still a small boy, Winston displayed high imaginative powers. Already in his youth he showed that natural courtesy and politeness to tenants, servants, and other dependents that was the hallmark of the gentleman in Victorian days. Everyone fell under the spell of Master Winston. Only his father was still skeptical. He called his elder son a "dunce" — but "a good 'un . . . a good 'un . . ." he assured his friends.

At the age of twelve, Winston declared firmly: "Of course I will become a soldier while there is any fighting to be done. After that I will have a shot at politics."

The two cousins

Lord Randolph
Churchill

WINSTON spent three of his four and a half years at Harrow in the Army class. It was preparation for Sandhurst, the Academy for gentlemen cadets. There he became a celebrated horseman, and an excellent fencer. Moreover, he soon led his class in Tactics and Fortifications, the two most important subjects.

No longer worried about his son's future, Lord Randolph traveled to South Africa. The gold rush in Johannesburg was just on, and Lord Randolph returned £7,000 richer. But his health was irreparably shattered. He grew a wild, grayish beard, and became increasingly impatient and irritable. His wife suggested a journey around the world. It would, she realized, probably be his journey into death. But if his fate was sealed, the restless seeker for excitement should not linger; he should fall, quickly and painlessly, in a last gallop. The nearer euthanasia approached Lord Randolph, the sharper grew his perception, the more intense became his morbid desire to see everything, to meet everyone, to take along at least the memories.

The Churchills' medical practitioner accompanied the pair. It was frequently asserted, but never confirmed, that the doctor had a coffin among his luggage.

In Bombay, already on their way home, Lord Randolph collapsed. In a state of near coma he still reached his mother's house in London, 50, Grosvenor Square. On January 24, at 6:25 in the morning, he passed away, exactly as Lady Randolph had prayed for — gently, painlessly, as if he were falling into slumber.

Winston kept guard at his father's deathbed. Eyewitnesses reported his expression of strong determination. He would now be his father's executor.

THE DEATH of his father cast a dark shadow on what was otherwise Winston's most joyful period of youth. He had become Sub-Lieutenant in the Fourth, The Queen's Own, Hussars, one of the proudest British cavalry regiments. Both the warrior cub and the artist in him delighted in the thrill and the charm in the glittering jingle of a cavalry squadron maneuvering at the trot. The stir of the horses, the clank of their equipment, the thrill of motion, the tossing plumes, the sense of incorporation in a living machine, the suave dignity of the uniform — all these, in Mr. Churchill's own words, intoxicated him. His only regret was that he would never in his time see a war.

Sub-Lieutenant in the
Fourth Hussars (*European*)

Gentleman cadet

IN CUBA, at least a revolution was on. Winston had ten weeks' leave from the army coming. His mother obtained his first newspaper assignment as a war correspondent: five articles, at five pounds each. (The time he drew $2,500 for an article was still to come.) Early in November, 1895, he embarked for Havana. Although only a civilian newspaperman during his leave from the Fourth Hussars, he plunged instantly into the thick of the fight. He was accredited to Spanish headquarters, and while he dined there with the son of the Duke of Tetuan, explaining to the grandee why he, Winston Churchill, sympathized with the revolutionaries, a band of guerrillas assailed Royal Headquarters. They were beaten back. Elated, Winston grinned. Real bullets whistling around his head! He was not hurt, but he was "blooded."

THE knight-errant's next stop was India. In late autumn, 1896, a troopship
with 1,200 men sailed from Southampton to Bombay in twenty-three days.
Churchill, going at his habitual furious pace, could not wait to feel again
firm land under his feet. He jumped ashore from his little landing craft so
violently and unluckily that he smashed his right shoulder, already injured
by a childhood accident. By Jove, what was to become of his polo career
in the Indian Army?

He accomplished other things in India, too. He fought the wild Pathan
tribesmen, in the present war some of the most courageous soldiers in the
White Emperor's Army. He joined the utmost advance guard of the Bengal
Lancers to share in hand-to-hand fights with the wild Mamunds, whose
sons and grandsons are today heavily engaged with the Japs in Burma.
He sent articles from the front to the *Daily Telegraph,* always ahead of the
Intelligence Service's reports. He had advance information in the truest
sense of the word. "Churchill was out all day," Colonel, later Field Marshal,
Ian Hamilton recorded, "stalking the enemy snipers, or relieving some
picket whose position seemed open for bloodshed. At night he wrote
copiously." Indeed, in the thick of the fight, he produced *The Malakand
Field Force,* a military classic in two volumes.

But his real achievement was polo. The tournament for the Golconda
cup took place at Hyderabad. The Golconda Brigade, the bodyguard of
the Nizam of Hyderabad, were sure-fire winners. All India bet on the
"killers." Winston Churchill, still with a fractured right shoulder, and
smelling of blood and powder, in the center of the team of the Fourth
Hussars, beat the "killers" nine to three, then all the other teams.

The Sirdar

AND so to the Sudan, to join the Sirdar's campaign against the dervishes. Winston was attached as Supernumerary Lieutenant to the 21st Lancers. Kitchener had refused him a commission in his own Egyptian Army. He resented the young subaltern who wrote fault-finding reports and sharply critical books about colonial wars. Churchill, however, found a niche in the British contingent that assisted Kitchener's army.

The 21st Lancers formed the spearhead of the army marching upon Omdurman, the dry-mud residence of the Caliph. On August 15 the regiment crossed the left bank of the Nile at its confluence with the Arbara. Nine days of perilous desert march followed. At the camp north of the Shabluka Cataract the advance group detached itself to proceed alone. The group was led by Reconnaissance-Officer Lieutenant Churchill.

Nothing happened for a whole week. On the first of September, however, the handful of Lancers of the advance group saw the enemy approaching. Their main body settled down opposite the Lancers, at a distance of about seven miles. Lieutenant Churchill's heart beat rapidly. For the first time he felt something like fear. He did not, of course, mind a few thousand howling dervishes opposite. He was terrified that he, the reconnaissance-officer, would now have to report to, and hence meet, Kitchener, whose powerful infantry columns, under the Union Jack and the Egyptian flag, were already rolling on.

Churchill galloped to deliver his message to the Sirdar. Quietly the Field Marshal asked: "How much time have I left?" "An hour . . . or an hour and a half," Churchill replied, pulling himself together. This was, he recalled years later, his whole contribution to the grand strategy of Omdurman.

21

Lieutenant
Winston S. Churchill,
attached to 21st Lancers

HE contributed more to the fight. In the twenty minutes that live on in history as the cavalry charge of Omdurman, Winston Churchill was the first officer in the rank. The Lancers attacked — it was the great charge every cavalryman had been dreaming about during the whole campaign — and the dervishes flung themselves among the white devils' horses. The first two enemies fired at Churchill at a distance of about ten yards. He was not hurt. But a Lancer behind him fell from his horse. Winston's pony galloped to a ditch to seek cover. The ditch was full of dervishes. Churchill had to shoot his way out with his Mauser pistol. Even the wounded among the dervishes fought savagely. They attacked the Lancers with their swords. In the heat of the fight Winston had strayed away from his own troops. He was faced by a crowd of hostile horsemen. At this very moment brown Lancers uniforms appeared at the rear of the dervishes. Winston plunged headlong into the fray. The savages were already in full flight. Twenty minutes after the charge had started, the Caliphate disappeared without leaving a trace.

Now Churchill's hunger for battle was satisfied. Writing was a much better and more important proposition. He could make a living with his pen, but not on his ridiculously small lieutenant's salary. Nor could he continue accepting his mother's allowance of £500 annually. Lady Randolph had nothing left but her dowry. And if it costs money to be a beautiful woman, it costs more to remain a beautiful woman.

On July 7, Winston Churchill took off his red coat. Going to the wars again? No, thank you! Never more!

The greatest and the latest correspondent of the day with
Lord Leslie, British Military Censor

OOM PAUL'S ultimatum to the British Empire had been known for less
than an hour in London when Winston had a contract with Mr. Borthwick,
publisher of the *Morning Post*, in his pocket — this time at the rate of
£250 a month. At twenty-five he was the highest-paid English war correspondent of his time. He arrived at the field of battle on October 31, 1899,
precisely nineteen days after the invasion of the Natal Colony, British
territory, by the Boer general, Joubert. His daily cable to the *Morning Post*
was the sensation of London — although there were only initial reverses to
report. They were wired back to the English-language press in South
Africa. Within two weeks the young man in a hurry was recognized as
the "greatest and the latest correspondent of the day."

Exactly on the fourteenth day of his assignment, somewhere between
Chieveley Station and Estcourt, he was taken prisoner by the Boers, while
accompanying a makeshift British armored train. Boer guerrillas had cut
the rails. Their commando waylaid the stranded English soldiers.

23

DESPITE his perfectly correct protest that he was unarmed and a civilian by status, the Boers transported him into the Pretoria Model Schools, where captured British officers were kept. His treatment was perfect; his food, in the best Boer manner, rough and ready and much too plentiful. But Winston felt only cramped. He sent a letter of protest, explaining his case, to the State Attorney, a promising young Advocate by the name of Smuts, who refused with four curt words: "Winston Churchill non-combatant? Impossible." But Churchill had already escaped.

HOW WINSTON SPENCER CHURCHILL ESCAPED

1. The place where the British prisoners are confined in Pretoria is surrounded by a high wall. Watching his opportunity when one of the Boer guards had turned his back, Winston Spencer Churchill seized the moment for escape, and leapt the fence with one quick bound.

2. It was some time before he reached the open country, and then he was so fortunate as to meet a goods train. Into one of the trucks he clambered, and pulled the heavy sacks of coal over to conceal himself. In this terrible position he lay for hours, not daring to move, for he knew he was pursued.

3. Though the train was searched, he could not be found, and jumping from the train, he spent the night in the woods, with a vulture for a companion. The bird seemed much interested in him, wondering, perhaps, whether it would yet wet its beak on the runaway.

ON DECEMBER 30 the following newspaper story appeared:

DEC. 30, 18:9.   PEARSON'S   ILLUSTRATED   WAR   NEWS.   3

HOW I ESCAPED
FROM PRETORIA.

By Winston Churchill.

THE *Morning Post* has received the following telegram from Mr. Winston Spencer Churchill, its war correspondent, who was taken prisoner by the Boers and escaped from Pretoria.

LOURENÇO MARQUES, December 21st, 10 p.m.

I was concealed in a railway truck under great sacks.

I had a small store of good water with me.

I remained hidden, chancing discovery.

The Boers searched the train at Komati Poort, but did not search deep enough, so after sixty hours of misery I came safely here.

I am very weak, but I am free.

I have lost many pounds weight, but I am lighter in heart.

I shall also avail myself of every opportunity from this moment to urge with earnestness an unflinching and uncompromising prosecution of the war.

On the afternoon of the 12th the Transvaal Government's Secretary for War informed me that there was little chance of my release.

I therefore resolved to escape the same night, and left the State Schools Prison at Pretoria by climbing the wall when the sentries' backs were turned momentarily.

I walked through the streets of the town without any disguise, meeting many burghers, but I was not challenged in the crowd.

I got through the pickets of the Town Guard, and struck the Delagoa Bay Railroad.

I walked along it, evading the watchers at the bridges and culverts.

I waited for a train beyond the first station.

The out 11.10 goods train from Pretoria arrived, and before it had reached full speed I boarded with great difficulty, and hid myself under coal sacks.

I jumped from the train before dawn, and sheltered during the day in a small wood, in company with a huge vulture, who displayed a lively interest in me.

I walked on at dusk.

There were no more trains that night.

The danger of meeting the guards of the railway line continued; but I was obliged to follow it, as I had no compass or map.

I had to make wide *détours* to avoid the bridges, stations, and huts.

The outlook was gloomy, but I persevered, with God's help, for five days.

The food I had to have was very precarious.

I was lying up at daylight, and walking on at night time, and, meanwhile, my escape had been discovered and my description telegraphed everywhere.

All the trains were searched.

Everyone was on the watch for me.

Four wrong people were arrested.

But on the sixth day I managed to board a train beyond Middleburg, whence there is a direct service to Delagoa.

Escape of Mr. Winston Churchill from Pretoria: He spends a day with a vulture. (*Pearson's War Magazine*)

SUBSEQUENTLY he told his story to lecture audiences on both sides of the Atlantic, winning new fame in America, increasing his popularity in England, and earning handsome lecture fees. His magic lantern dramatized the highlights of his adventure.

For a day and a night, he recalled, a vulture circled him, fluttering ever closer around the exhausted man. But Winston escaped once more.

Winston Churchill landing at Durban after his escape. (*Pearson's War Magazine*)

FINALLY he made friends. One of them, a good-natured Dutch merchant, was shipping wool bales to Delagoa Bay, the Portuguese harbor. One wool bale contained "the greatest and the latest correspondent of the day." Winston sailed to Durban ——

— to fall right into the arms of his indefatigable mother, who had equipped the American hospital ship *Maine* to bring relief and comfort to the wounded, probably also to have a glance at her two sons, both busy in South Africa — Winston in his "peaceful" occupation.

All's well that ends well? There was a fly in the ointment. Winston was shocked when he saw a Boer Proclamation offering £25 for his capture, dead or alive. His brilliant head worth no more than a shabby twenty-five quid?

Facsimile of the Boer Proclamation for the capture of Mr. Winston Churchill

AND NOW, at twenty-six, he had his "shot at politics," announced fourteen years before. In fact, it was his second shot. The first one had been a dud. Already between the Sudan campaign and the Boer War he had tried his hand in a by-election. Barely three months after his feats at Omdurman, he had visited the Conservative chief whip, Mr. Middleton, "the skipper," and had bashfully alluded to his political ambitions. It so happened that a by-election in Oldham was approaching at that time. English by-elections were a sort of Fools' Fair. The cranks and faddists from all over the country congregated to let off steam. Moreover, Oldham was notoriously the most fickle constituency in radical Lancashire, the county whence the industrial revolution sprang. Young Churchill was beaten by a hundred-odd votes.

But now, after his glorious escape from prison in Pretoria, it was a different matter. When last year's defeated candidate marched into Old-

Honorable Winston Spencer Churchill (*Photo by Thomson*)

ham with a procession of ten landaus, the streets of the town were packed with workers and mill girls. "God bless Churchill, England's noblest hero!" a banner, hung across the main street, greeted him. "See, the conquering hero comes!" the band played over and over again. He had won the race before he began to speak. He entered the House, and thus history, on January 23, 1901.

Reviving "a certain splendid memory" (*Punch*)

ON FEBRUARY 27, 1901, late in the evening, Winston Churchill, Conservative M. P., delivered his maiden speech. The House received him with high expectation, although he was still personally unknown to two-thirds of the members. Lloyd George, a young Welsh solicitor in a shabby, rumpled suit, had spoken before him, mercilessly attacking the Boer War and England's accursed Imperialism as well.

In the midst of the tension created by Lloyd George's harangue, Churchill rose from his corner seat behind the Treasury Bench. No friendly cheers greeted the newcomer. But before his third sentence, he caught the attention of his audience, growing keener and kinder when, in reply to whispered questions, the answer went around, "Lord Randolph's son!" Winston himself alluded in a delicate touch to "a certain splendid memory." Although nothing in his voice or manner recalled his father, he had the same command of the pointed phrase, and the same self-possession verging perhaps on self-assurance. (He had prepared, and learned by heart, a half-dozen speeches to meet any emergency.) He also had inherited Lord Randolph's gift of viewing familiar topics from new standpoints, as well as his shrewd, confident judgment.

Lord Hugh Cecil: Uncompromising supporter of conservative tradition, champion of Church, State and Free Trade (*Elliot and Fry*)

HIS earliest years in Parliament, Mr. Churchill recollected, were lived within the orbit of Lord Hugh Cecil: a real Tory, a being out of the Seventeenth century, equipped with every modern convenience and aptitude. Lord Hugh is a scion of the Cecils, one of the great houses that gave England her leading statesmen for many a century, the son of Lord Salisbury, who for twenty years was Prime Minister. Today Lord Hugh Cecil is a don in Oxford. His name is Baron Quickswood.

31

"WINSTON." "A tortured face weighted with the cares of Empire"

WINSTON delivered his maiden speech in the midst of the Boer War debate. He pleaded for a full account of the operations. "I have in many cases myself supplied the only report given to the country on some important matter," he said, referring to his correspondence in the *Morning Post*. He continued: "I feel keenly the responsibility which has thus been placed upon me, and I think it is time for the Secretary for War to relieve me of some of it." Whereupon Herbert Asquith spoke of "that burden of responsibility that at present weighs so heavily on the honorable member's shoulders." With this fine touch of irony, the Liberal leader found the weak place in Churchill's heart. The Benjamin of Parliament was burning to shoulder some of the responsibility.

Mr. Winston Spencer Churchill, M.P.
(*A caricature sketch from the Press Gallery*)

THE BOER WAR lingered on, although ultimate British victory was now assured. Yet Botha and Smuts were still in the field, the latter as an eminently successful guerrilla raider. Mr. Broderick, as Secretary of War responsible for the Empire's defense, had learned his lesson. He presented his Army Estimates by which six new corps were to be organized, three of them always ready for service abroad. This demand was modest, but grandiose in its conception to make England army-conscious.

Winston Churchill was for a vigorous fight to the finish, but for immediate reconciliation as soon as the guns were silenced. However, he was not of a mind to let Mr. Broderick get away with "planned Imperialism."

As soon as the Army Estimates were presented Churchill was on his feet, delivering a fiery anti-militarist speech that echoed throughout the kingdom: "The House cannot view without grave apprehension the continual growth of purely military expenditure. The House desires to postpone the final decision on future military policy until calmer times!"

IT WAS the voice of Lord Randolph speaking from the grave. The Conservatives displayed open hostility against their rebellious member. They had to listen resentfully to such words as these: "It is a great mistake to spend thirty millions a year on the army. One corps is enough to fight savages, and six are not enough to fight Europeans. After victory in South Africa we must cut down military expenditure. I refer to the half-forgotten episode of my father's fall. Then the Government triumphed. The Chancellor of the Exchequer went down forever, and with him, as it now seems, there fell also the cause of retrenchment and economy, so that the words themselves now have a curiously old-fashioned ring."

The baby of the House conjured up the good old days. Wasn't it plain irony? But the irony lay deeper than Winston himself understood. "I am glad that the House has allowed me to lift again the tattered flag of retrenchment and economy — the tattered flag I found lying on a stricken field!" Was this the language of an anti-militarist or of a swashbuckler from the Hussars? The sudden arch-pacifist was, of course, a born fighter, even if now a white banner fluttered ahead of him. It was the fighting son, raising the shield of his fallen father in the midst of the battle.

In his highest combative mood he found a few words truly prophetic in the spring of 1901: "Now when mighty populations are impelled on each other, when the resources of science sweep away everything that might mitigate the nations' fury, a European war can only end in the ruin of the vanquished and the scarcely less fatal exhaustion of the conquerors. The wars of people will be more terrible than the wars of kings."

THE twenty-six-year-old junior member for Oldham was a generation ahead of his time. He was the first to raise the question of the future of mankind. But he could not find the right answer in his days of storm and stress. "The honor and security of the British Empire do not depend, and can never depend, on the British Army!" he cried out in his frightful confusion of feelings.

"Willful mutiny!" the Conservatives replied. "Please go!" they challenged him, without forgetting the "please." The Liberals licked their lips. Massingham, their journalist spokesman, commented: "The author of this speech will be Prime Minister—Liberal Prime Minister, I hope, of England."

At an early division Churchill was the only Conservative member to vote against Broderick's Army Reform Scheme. But a great many people in the country were with him. The British lion only roars when someone twists his tail. The easy-going ways of a fundamentally unmilitary nation were his natural allies. Winston Churchill grew popular with astonishing speed. His anti-militaristic speeches goaded the country to a frenzy. Not even the relegation of Mr. Broderick to the much less controversial India Office in a cabinet reshuffle could stop him.

This reshuffle occurred when Lord Salisbury, at last, after twenty years of brilliant leadership, had to resign for reasons of age and health. His nephew and successor, Mr. Arthur Balfour, once a detached fellow-traveler of Lord Randolph's Tory democracy, was generally expected to find some minor government post for the hero of Pretoria and the junior member of Oldham. But Mr. Balfour brushed Winston Churchill aside.

MR. WINSTON CHURCHILL AND MR. BALFOUR. Mr. Balfour: "Confound that boy! He's always doing something weird!"

(*Westminster Gazette*, February, 1902)

35

MR. ARTHUR BALFOUR, perfect embodiment of Conservatism, grew weary of the erratic "young man of promise — and of promises." When Churchill at last crossed the gangway, Mr. Balfour, of course, was too polite to shrug. But he showed no signs of regret. Remarkably enough, great old Chamberlain — whose switch to Protection was the straw that broke the camel's back and exhausted Winston's "patience"— said to Margot Asquith: "Winston is the cleverest of all the young men. The mistake Arthur made was to let him go."

This remark was made on June 1, 1903, the day after the evening Winston had a drink at the bar of the House, to raise his courage before he entered the chamber, and walked to his old seat below the gangway. He stared fixedly at the opposite side. He bowed to the Speaker, faced sharply about, and strode stiffly to an empty seat beside Lloyd George. It was great showmanship. The rumpled Welsh solicitor, the gadfly of the House, half rose to welcome the new convert to Liberalism. A life-long friendship between the two fire-eaters began, full of mutual admiration, and spiced with a good portion of malice.

WINSTON continued his one-man campaign. Fundamentally, it did not agree with him. The *Daily Mail* remarked: "Already Mr. Churchill's head is carried with a droop. He drops it forward as if it were heavy. That is what you see in one moment — a pose prophetic of what is too likely to fasten itself upon him before he reaches middle age."

Churchill in Parliament
37

A Humbert Patent.

Disrespectful boy: "It's all rot! There's nothing inside." "He had felt convinced that the great French fraud at which we had been amused was merely a poor, wretched, private concern compared to the great English fraud which the War Office was perpetrating every day." Mr. Winston Churchill at Wallsend, February 12, 1903.

(*Westminster Gazette, February, 1903*)

WINSTON CHURCHILL went from bad to worse. Obviously to increase his vote-getting capacity with the workingmen's district of Oldham, he told his constituents: "I regard it a grave mistake in Imperial policy to spend thirty millions a year on the army. I hold that the continual increase in army expenditure cannot be viewed by supporters of the Government without the greatest alarm and apprehension, and by members who represent working-class districts without extreme dislike."

He surpassed himself on February 12, 1903, at a time when the whole world spoke about the "great French fraud," by describing the Army Reform to the voters of Wallsend as "The Great English Fraud."

An American lady
in Europe (*After an
original painting by
Hal Hurst*)

WINSTON'S defection heralded a total split among the Conservatives. His personal fate, as well as his rabid pretend-anti-militarism left his former party colleagues ice-cold. Unanimously they felt relieved from his presence. Only one particularly irate Tory exclaimed: "Winston . . . there is nothing in Winston. But he has got some of the cleverest women in England behind his back. That's the real secret of his success." Another old member agreed: "When I see him I must always think of a Chicago newsboy. He owes it to his American strain which comes from his mother," the worthy divulged. "From her he inherited the full measure of his American snap. He is a first-class hustler, pushing as a New England canvasser. He has beaten his rivals by his American ways. He means to make things hum. He is constantly on the alert: never silent, neither in the House, nor in the country."

Mr. Winston Churchill, M.P. (*Photo by E. H. Mills*)

IT WAS not this storm in the teacup, it was Chamberlain's fight for tariffs, that pitted Tories against Tories. Mr. Arthur Balfour took no sides. Yet he had to reconstruct his short-lived first cabinet. A general election was inevitable. No doubt a landslide would sweep away the Conservatives.

Churchill went through his first serious crisis. His departure from the hereditary Conservative Party was a leap in the dark. He had lost the support of his highly influential paternal family, indeed, his natural stay. Why did he take this grave risk? The Conservatives themselves had shelved Mr. Broderick's plan. The Tariff question was by no means decided, and Churchill could have used his influence to much better purpose inside the ruling camp than on the opposition bench. The real reason for his breach with his natural surrounding was deeper than all that. He would no longer accept the Conservative tradition: "Young men can wait!"

With the extremism of a convert, he became the spearhead of every attack against the fading Conservative majority. His radical views were popular: the country was weary of the long Tory rule. Churchill won a triumphal majority in Manchester, which caused the special correspondent of the violently anti-Churchill *Daily Mail* to report: "Grand slam in doubled no trumps."

WINSTON became Under-Secretary for the Colonies in Campbell-Bannerman's Liberal government. He remained in the Colonial Office for a first term of twenty years, with a few months' interruption. He had taken the first step on the ladder. But he felt uncomfortable, exhausted, not very proud of the methods with which he had greatly helped his party win the polls, perturbed by the absurdity of his hot, red, or rather rouged, anti-militarism. Writing and golf kept him fit. He was a hard-hitting player.

Winston at the tee

Winston grinning at the Conservatives
(*Caricature by Cosmo Hamilton*)

CHURCHILL joined a Leftish government whose political merits will remain controversial. Its literary distinction, however, no one can deny. His new colleagues included four famous writers: John Morley, James Bryce, Augustine Birrell, and Richard Burdon Haldane. He was in excellent aesthetic and philosophic company. Besides, he instantly proved himself a brilliant and enthusiastic administrator. With an aside to the Conservatives, who had lost him, he grinned, perhaps a bit too cheerful to be true.

Winston at his literary labors

HE SPENT his nights secluded in his flat in Mount Street, working on his father's biography. It was a tremendous job. The research compelled the author to devour thousands of letters and documents. Then came a thousand-odd longhand written pages of text.

Love's labor was not lost. *The Life of Lord Randolph Churchill* became a monumental work, and to this day belongs with the English political classics. The readers were astonished that Winston's apology for his father was as punctiliously impartial as it proved to be. It was written with full respect for Lord Randolph's antagonists. Finally, the filial author, though not concealing his own strong feelings, abstained from any judgment. Presenting the intimate but scrupulously documented facts, he invited the English people to form their own opinions. As a result, Lord Randolph was certainly better understood after his death than throughout his lifetime.

A welcome by-product of the book's success was the material reward. Winston did not yet receive Kipling's rates. But he got £8,000 advance, and a further 50 per cent interest after the publisher's earnings would have yielded £12,000.

The Critic, a literary magazine, concluded its review of the book with the statement: "No English man of politics has made such rapid strides toward a predominant position as Winston Churchill during the last few months. Recognizing the tireless energy and varied ability of this young man, it is quite likely that even his work in the Colonial Office and his fame as a brilliant debater in the House may only be incidental to his literary career."

HIS VERSATILE character and his magnetic charms served him well in his first office. Winston's laugh was unlike anyone else's. It was, indeed, infectious. At a public meeting he used to share in the merriment incited by his own jests, which did no harm to his popularity. In private life, however, there was no need to lend a helping grin. Everyone chuckled at his subtle and prematurely wise humor. No one else possessed Winston's facility for self-teasing. As a young man he never displayed the same humor twice, but always he was entertaining, good-natured, and encouraging to everyone. His speeches were well rehearsed and carefully polished. Yet his quip, "Mr. Chamberlain loves the working man, he loves to see him work," sounded completely spontaneous.

Now in the Liberal Party, but never of the Liberal Party, the man who already in his youth blasted any party frame, worked off his inner dilemma by stressing the party's supreme importance. To a young gate crasher, who wished to enter the House as an independent supporter of Winston Churchill, he replied portentously: "This is an age of the party machine. Unless you belong to one or the other of the recognized parties you will in nine hundred ninety-nine out of a thousand cases not have a ghost of a chance."

Winston had an answer for everything and to everyone. Particularly during question time, he used to flourish like rich grass in a heavy rainfall.

ONE STEP NEARER.
With congratulations to the Right Honorable Winston Churchill. P. C. (*Punch*)

TOWARD the middle of April, 1907, the Under-Secretary became a Privy Councillor.

"Judging Character by Correspondence": or, The Winston Touch.
Our artist has curiously few opportunities of attending Cabinet Councils, but, after a careful study of Mr. Winston Churchill's letter to his constituents about the "8" (Dreadnoughts) question, in which he lightheartedly castigates every axiom and argument of his dear colleagues, he feels sure that the above can be no inaccurate representation of what usually occurs when the Cabinet meets in council.   (*Punch*)

RIGHTLY, he could now feel himself the equal of his senior colleagues. He addressed an open letter to his constituents severely criticizing a planned modest increase in the Royal Navy. Now safely entrenched on the wrong side, he became the holy terror of his cabinet colleagues.

THE old-fashioned cavalier and immortal cavalryman in him was, of course, disgusted with the tutelage of the petty Welsh solicitor in his crumpled suit, with having to court underpaid and undernourished voters, and all the other duties of a budding man of politics who could, unfortunately, not choose another way to his impatiently awaited complete self-assertion.

For a few hot midsummer days of 1906 he felt released from all this drudgery. The German Crown Prince, with whom Winston had recently played billiards, had returned to Potsdam full of praise of his partner. Like his predecessor, Frederick the Great, and like his successor, that man . . . , Wilhelm II was possessed by an insatiable zest to draw all the stars on the European firmament to his court. The anointed histrion was, of course, fully aware that he looked his best in his Field Marshal's regalia.

Churchill at the German Army's summer maneuvers in 1906

He sent a personal invitation to the British Under-Secretary of Colonies, the famed warrior, to visit the German summer maneuvers.

Churchill enjoyed the brief holiday tremendously. For a short time he was not torn by his dilemma. As a Leftist, he knew, he would do some good by making friends with the German Emperor. His Rightist self relished "the stir of the horses, the clank of their equipment, the thrill of motion, the tossing plumes, the sense of incorporation in a living machine, the suave dignity of the uniform." Disdaining the offered motorcar, one of the newest products of German ingenuity — or so the Kaiser maintained—Churchill preferred to watch on horseback the review of irresistible German power.

47

Churchill advising Wilhelm II, after the German Army maneuvres,
according to Mr. Punch   (*Punch*)

AFTER the maneuvers, Wilhelm II and Winston Churchill had a heart-to-heart talk. Winston was duly impressed by the military show, but by no means awe-stricken. Particularly the German cavalry, though formidable, seemed second-class when the beloved shades of Sandhurst arose, and when he felt, as it were, the powder in the hot air of the 21st Lancers' charge at Omdurman.

48

As a good-will ambassador, however, he was perfectly ready to give the Emperor a piece of his mind. Mr. Punch listened in. Here, in his words, is what Winston had to say to His Majesty:

"Now mind, Your Majesty, if any point should arise during the manoeuvres that you don't quite understand — that you can't get the hang of — don't hesitate to ask me. Remember, I shall never be thinking too deeply to be disturbed by you. Any topic, mind! Strategy or tactics, anything that worries you about the Empire — all the same to me, you know — put you right in a moment."

Young Winston looks into the mirror. (*Punch*)

The Liberal — Mr. Winston Churchill

SO WINSTON CHURCHILL returned to the dreariness of his early triumphs. Fortunately, he soon fell up the ladder. Campbell Bannerman succumbed in April, 1908. Herbert Henry Asquith became his successor, the last in the line of the classic British statesmen-philosophers. In his newly formed cabinet he promoted Churchill to the rank of President of the Board of Trade. At that time a change of portfolio implied a by-election. With his habitual radiant confidence, Winston once again contested his own bailiwick in Manchester, where all the men that counted were under his spell.

BUT WINSTON had not reckoned with the women. Suffragettes ran riot. The target of their hysterical hatred and of many a combative parasol was Mr. Churchill, next to Prime Minister Asquith the chief opponent of votes for women, on the grounds that there should at least remain one group of people in England whom he had not to flatter, court, and woo. Of necessity, this group consisted of the English women—as long as they were denied the vote.

Winston Churchill was never a misogynist. He was "agin" no group or class of mankind. But, notwithstanding some gossip to the contrary, he was too deeply absorbed by his political obsession to find any interest in private ones. He was no "partie." Besides, he had inherited another trait from his father: he was a poor dancer.

The irate women of Manchester did, indeed, prevent Churchill from being returned. Many tired husbands, more interested in domestic peace than in political squabble, yielded, as was their habit, to their homemakers' wishes. Mr. Joynson-Hicks, a churchman and rigid Sabbatarian, won by some 500 votes.

Immediately the Liberal organization in Dundee offered Winston a seat which was just becoming free because its holder, Mr. Robinson, was about to enter the House of Lords. If it had been riot in Manchester, it was battle in Dundee. The Manchester amazons pursued Winston as far as Scotland. Here they encountered Mr. Scrimgeour, whose life's ambition it was to dry up Dundee, at that time reputed as "the drunkenest town in Scotland." At that, he had once seen a widely circulating cartoon: Winston

Churchill: "The most interesting addition to the
new Government"

51

Churchill sitting on the Treasury Bench in pink pyjamas. Only a drunkard could behave like this, Mr. Scrimgeour shrewdly concluded. When this drunkard dared to contest Dundee, Scrimgeour's holy fury and the furies from Manchester formed a formidable and vocal alliance.

One white-haired lady broke up this alliance. The Countess of Airlie, one of the Ogilvys, was the uncrowned Queen of Dundee. Her benevolence and charity had been legendary for many years. Since her daughter, Lady Blanche Hozier, was an intimate friend of Lady Randolph, the Countess' influence was completely at Churchill's disposal. The Countess offered the Liberal candidate her house as headquarters. Scores of radical workers flocked in, most of them somewhat embarrassed, but unabashed in their curiosity to have a look at, and a word with, Winston, the champ.

Churchill won the battle of Dundee by 7,000 votes against 4,000. The London press called him "the most interesting addition to the new Government."

Churchill and his mother (*Black and White*)

LADY RANDOLPH heartily enjoyed her son's success. Yet she worried for fear he would kill himself in his race. She was fully aware of the fact that her own influence on him no longer prevailed. Now they were brother and sister, not mother and son. Winston stood badly in need of a new manager. She decided to marry him off.

The Honorable Clementine Hozier (*Sphere*)

THERE was no question about her choice. With the instinct of a woman who herself had played a decisive role in the lives of two men, she singled out The Honorable Clementine Hozier, daughter of her friend Lady Blanche and the late Colonel H. M. Hozier, K. C. B.

Colonel H. M. Hozier, K.C.B. (*Windsor*)

54

WINSTON'S late father-in-law, although completely forgotten by history, was so remarkable a man that he certainly rates a short epitaph. A descendant of a well-known Lanarkshire family, of which Lord Newlands was head at that time, he was, of course, destined for a military career. He studied at Woolwich Academy, and took to the scientific branch of soldiering. But a long time elapsed before he received a commission in the artillery. Most of this time he spent in Paris, studying medicine. Later in life he said with a smile: "I would not wish my worst enemy to consult me as a doctor."

At long last he received his commission. He was dispatched with a battery to China, where he fought in several campaigns for seven years. Thus began his time of adventure. Upon his return to England the over-age lieutenant was transferred to the Staff College. From there he joined the 2nd Life Guards.

Like Winston, he was a journalist-officer, probably the first. His articles on artillery attracted wide attention. Quickly he mounted the list. In 1866, *The Times* of London assigned him as a war correspondent on the Prussian side of the war with Austria. But the Prussians were suspicious. They would not let the English artillery expert cover the front. Hozier resorted to a ruse. He rushed to Berlin to offer the British Ambassador his good services as courier for His Excellency's confidential correspondence with the Prussian Crown Prince in the field.

Lord Adolfus Loftus was tickled to death. Of course he had no confidential correspondence whatsoever with Prussian royalty. But the mere thought that the *Times* correspondent thought so, rated Captain Hozier a solemn passport bearing the British arms and seal, which was to become a perfect *laissez-passer*.

In the next year Major Hozier accompanied Lord Napier as military secretary on an Abyssinian expedition. In 1870 he acted as British Military Attaché at Prussian headquarters. His return to the Intelligence Department crowned his military career.

IN 1894 Colonel Hozier resigned on the same grounds Winston Churchill took off his red coat: an officer could not make a living on his salary. The experienced administrator, the man of culture and intelligence, highly trained and developed by study and experience, the scientific soldier who had served in several regiments and in many climes, one of the earliest successful war correspondents, distinguished writer with many scholarly and entertaining books to his credit, a first-rate mathematician, fluent in a dozen foreign tongues, found easily a great position in business. The retired Colonel became the "Hozier of Lloyds."

Although Lloyds is generally identified with maritime business, few people realize how widespread are its working and control, how colossal are the interests the House watches over. Toward the end of the last century the pivot around which everything moved and happened was the secretary general, which post unassuming Colonel Hozier, retired, had chosen when he actually took over the general managership of the world business.

He remained entirely unchanged by his change in fortune. The typical Victorian worthy, full of "pawky" Scotch humor, yet also a man of masterful decision, born and trained to command, he divided his time between running Lloyds and his passion for charities. The Royal Alfred and the Seaman's Hospitals, the Children's Holiday Fund, and many more institutions owed him their foundation.

Colonel Hozier, retired, as "Hozier of Lloyds" (*Windsor*)

One of Miss Hozier's new gowns
(*Sphere*)
Another of Miss Hozier's new gowns
(*Sphere*)

WHEN he passed away, his widow and his daughter became inseparable companions. Clementine had spent a few years in Paris to receive her finishing education. When she appeared in her first London season, society called her a "stunner" — Edwardian for astonishing beauty.

Winston had met her first in Dundee. Just as in the case of his parents, it was love at first sight. A whirlwind courtship followed. Marriage was announced for September 12, 1908 — not quite five months after the battle of Dundee — at St. Margaret's, Westminster.

At her home in Abdington Villa, Kensington, The Honorable Clementine Hozier went through her dress rehearsal. The decisive moment was approaching.

The bride arriving with her brother, Sub-Lieutenant Hozier, at St. Margaret's (*Sphere*)

Winston in greatest hurry. The bridegroom alights at St. Margaret's, Westminster. (*Sphere*)

ALL London celebrated. Lord Hugh Cecil was best man. Gifts arrived from the King and Queen, and from a great many friends. The young couple spent their first days in Blenheim. Then they visited Lago Maggiore, and came home to settle down in London in Eccleston Square, Victoria.

Their wedding was the greatest adventure in both their lives. Neither had money. The young statesman was now too preoccupied with his official duties to add to his income by literary and journalistic work. He depended entirely on his "Office of Pay under the Crown" — an unreliable and inadequate source of income. "Clemmie" was completely unafraid. She knew that some tight spots now and then would be inevitable. But she would muddle through, and devote her life to managing Winston. "Managing Winston" is up to this day Mrs. Churchill's leitmotif.

"My most brilliant achievement," Winston Churchill summed up in later days, "was my ability to persuade my wife to marry me."

And so they were united, for better or for worse.

Mr. and Mrs. Winston Churchill. "My most brilliant achievement was my ability to persuade my wife to marry me"

YOUNG happiness is infectious. A short time after his older brother's wedding, Major John Strange Churchill gave up his man-about-town life to lead Lady Gwendolyne Bertie to the altar.

Major John Strange Churchill and his Bride, Lady Gwendolyne Bertie (*C. Vandyke*)

Winston and his bride on their daily morning ride in Rotten Row

(Elliot and Fry)

SOON after his wedding Winston Churchill resumed his work at break-
neck speed. Still, he found time to accompany his bride on their daily
morning ride in Rotten Row.

Campaigning at Southport (*Strand*)

CAMPAIGNING at Southport, soon after the wedding, Churchill, rushing to the train, grabbed an old, worn hat, a relic of his early youth, which his square-set head had long outgrown. A photographer caught the pair on the beach, and asked permission to take the candidate's picture. No candidate has ever refused such a request. Winston smiled straight into the lens.

Madame lowered her head, and smiled, rather embarrassed, at the sand. She tried to avoid the painful aspect of her husband's terrible hat.

From that day to the present, the tiny hat on his broad head is Mr. Churchill's trade-mark among cartoonists. At first he was a little angry about it. But for a long time Mr. Churchill has been well aware of the value of a personal symbol, preferably an amusing one, for the popularity of a man in public life. His collection of headgear, and his obvious relish at displaying them, has undoubtedly added another touch, a light one, to his world-wide fame.

Churchill and his family at the opening of a Labor Exchange

AS PRESIDENT of the Board of Trade he accomplished much of the progressive legislation he had advocated in the House. He introduced the Labor Exchange against unemployment, which was a tremendous, if very costly, step forward. He was so proud of his achievement that he used to take his family along to festive openings of new exchanges.

Churchill haranguing his constituents

THE MINERS, Licensing, Small Holdings, Old Age Pensions, and Education Bills, were all his personal achievements. England fast became socially the most advanced country in the world. Churchill and Lloyd George, not without a feeling of competition, drove progress on and on. After the Welsh solicitor, now Chancellor of the Exchequer, introduced his first budget, taking the breath away even of those members of the opposition who had expected the worst, Churchill delivered his own harangue to his constituents, outbidding good old Dave.

AT FIRST the House of Lords rejected Lloyd George's "crazy budget." Churchill, though not concerned with the Treasury, took up the gantlet. He carried his campaign against the upper House all over England. He slashed at Their Lordships, and equally fiercely against capital. "In the future," the President of the Board of Trade promised, "the tax collector will no longer ask, 'What have you got?' but, 'How did you get it?' "

These years of radical exuberance were also the years of Winston Churchill's sympathy for Germany. Shortly before his wedding he had visited for the second time German summer maneuvers. As he came back, he addressed a letter to the chairman of his party organization at Dundee, exposing the "four cardinal errors current in naval circles." The fourth, and to him most fundamental, error was "that any profound antagonism exists between England and Germany." He waged a vigorous campaign against the Naval Estimates of his fellow cabinet member, Mr. McKenna, First Lord of the Admiralty, who, in the spring of 1909, demanded the building of six dreadnoughts on account of the rapid expansion of the German fleet. "We want eight, and we won't wait!" replied patriotic choruses. In an open letter to his constituents Mr. Churchill was quite satisfied with four.

This was Mr. Punch's answer:

Mr. Punch looks at
Mr. Churchill's German sympathies (*Punch*)

Churchill as Home Secretary

AS USUAL, Mr. Punch expressed the average Englishman's feeling. England was deeply peace-minded. No one expected a war. Yet Winston's sudden ultra-pacifism disturbed the pronounced English sense for balance and harmony. He had also overreached in his ferocious attacks on the Lords. No one wanted to lose a venerable, time-honored, peculiarly British institution.

Sympathy with the Lords was certainly one of the reasons why the next elections did not turn out favorably for the ruling Liberals. In Dundee, Churchill was returned. But the Liberals shrank to a one-man majority. There were now 275 of them in the Commons, against 274 Conservatives. A strong hand was needed to weather the storm. Churchill climbed another step on the ladder. He became Home Secretary.

HE MELLOWED in politics. He was progressive, no longer radical. He left the House of Lords severely alone. Soon after the birth of his first child, his daughter Sarah, he addressed audiences with one of his most trenchant phrases:

THE RIGHT HONORABLE WINSTON CHURCHILL, M.P.: "We are sure we shall do much more for the children who come after us, and who, when their turn comes, will look back to us with gratitude when they find they have to tread a smoother, a less stony, and a less adverse road."

THE CIVIL SERVICE called the new chief a slave driver. It was a typical English expression for the general approval which met the uncommonly hard-working and very efficient new minister. Both the Home Office and Scotland Yard were unanimous in his praise. Churchill, in turn, was deeply concerned with the well-being of the men entrusted to him. One of his first measures in the Home Office was a Prison Reform which made life in jail considerably easier. There is no doubt that he never forgot his own claustrophobia in the Pretoria prison.

On the other hand he showed deep concern for his own men, the bobbies. All over the United Kingdom he reviewed the police squads, looking at each man in the ranks with an expression of personal interest.

Churchill inspecting the police in Bristol

Winston is one of London's first citizens to patronize taxicabs

HE WAS equally progressive in his private life. The Home Secretary used his stately carriage only on official occasions. Citizen Winston Churchill was one of the first residents of London to patronize the taxicab.

BUT while Churchill mellowed in his domestic politics, his attitude toward Germany stiffened. He was still convinced that peace with Emperor Wilhelm was possible, and hence desirable. His awakening from the great illusion began during his first leave from the Home Office, which he spent aboard a friend's yacht, cruising the Mediterranean. In Constantinople the German Ambassador Marshal Baron Biberstein visited the yacht. Churchill tried to involve him in unofficial negotiations about the Berlin-Bagdad railway which Germany was building as a provocative expression of the *Drang nach dem Osten*. Churchill's cautious feeler met with a rude answer. The "panther leap" to Agadir followed, a German provocation of all Europe.

The insolence of this ruthless breach of international law set Churchill to thinking about his own affairs. Had he not ventured too far into the low-lands of party struggle? Was he a pacifist and radical first, or an English-man? Even Lloyd George began to see his own blindness. Churchill thought and acted at once. The Home Office was the first department to make preparations for war. Churchill signed a warrant permitting the opening of suspicious correspondence. This was infringing the privacy of corre-spondence. But Churchill's measure made available such intimate material about the German spy ring in the country that the latter could be rounded up to the last man at the beginning of the war.

Mr. Asquith was deeply impressed by the zeal of his young colleague. Late in October the Prime Minister invited his Home Secretary to a secret rendezvous "somewhere in Scotland." Asquith disclosed that war with Germany was inevitable. It was probable that the Kaiser would strike at England first, since the island had no strong army. "We have only the Navy," the Prime Minister concluded. "It is our only hope." Then, after a short pause, he asked the best man in his cabinet: "Would you like to go to the Admiralty?"

"Indeed I would!" Churchill answered quietly.

Part Two

THE VOICE OF ENGLAND

The First Lord returns from his investiture audience with the King.

A FEW weeks before his thirty-seventh birthday Winston Churchill had outgrown his youth. Now he was entirely through with ambitions, relish of offices, the craving for success. He no longer yearned for publicity. His ardent campaigning did not cease; indeed, it never ceased. But from the moment he assumed the post of First Lord of the Admiralty he was no longer the seat-hunter who courted constituents. His was the voice of England that resounded, with organ tones, to awake first his nation, and later the world. When he returned from his investiture audience with the King, he was a man devoted to the single cause he has pursued ever since.

Winston shows the Premier how to splice the main brace (*Punch*)

CHURCHILL'S appointment to the First Lordship was jubilantly welcomed — everywhere save in two quarters. Berlin raged about the "turncoat." He had endeared himself to the two leading members of the House of Hohenzollern. Twice he had offered a "Naval Holiday." (Neither of these offers had been deigned an answer by Tirpitz.) Moreover, his ferocious anti-militarism and fight against increases in the Naval Estimates was lingering on in the inflexible German mind.

Strange bedfellows — the Royal Navy did not take their new chief to their hearts, either. They resented the sweeping changes in almost all high positions and commands that Churchill immediately made, and they grumbled at being subordinated to a "politician." Even wise but weak Prime Minister Asquith became suddenly afraid of the fanatic zeal with which his own choice plunged into his work: the task not only of reforming the Navy, but of saving the Isles five minutes before twelve.

Asquith's half-heartedness was the only impediment Churchill acknowledged. He invited his chief aboard the Admiralty yacht *Enchantress*, and there the "enchanter of the *Enchantress*," Winston's nickname at that time, explained to the Prime Minister the inner workings of the Navy. Invisibly, Mr. Punch sat in.

HELP came from a quarter from which it was least expected. *The Review of Reviews*, of London, in the liberal heyday an important organ of radical opinion that had applauded Winston's youthful vagaries and wildly attacked him after what was clearly, though never publicly announced, his conversion, came out with a sensational piece. "Belonging really to no party, Mr. Churchill is gifted with highest imagination, restless energy, and boundless capacity for making good. Some, even in the present Government, look askance at the First Lord. But the mass of public opinion is behind him to a surprising degree. There are too few statesmen who can grasp the grand policy for a century to come, and in naval matters it is those alone who count. Party is not wanted in the Navy. Mr. Churchill is of all parties, and of no party. Let him insist on an immediate program for the strengthening of our Fleet in the Mediterranean, and he will have earned praises of the nation, which is worth so much more than the fleeting approval or condemnation of a party or a party leader. Mr. Churchill has an opportunity to show that he is worthy to be permanent Minister of the Navy."

"Mr. Churchill has an opportunity to show that he is worthy to be permanent Minister of the Navy." *The Review of Reviews*, London.

MOST certainly Churchill grasped his opportunity with both hands. Ruthlessly he reorganized the Royal Navy from top to bottom. A Sisyphean work that would have taken fifteen years if carried out discreetly had to be done in a year and a half. From then on, the whole English Government knew — but failed to inform the nation for fear of creating panic, and losing its popularity — that Germany could attack England any day.

Churchill's iron broom swept clean the Navy from top to bottom. The first victim of his purge was his next highest in rank, Sir Arthur Wilson, First Sea Lord, an *anima candida,* completely unselfish and without the slightest personal ambitions. Unfortunately, Sir Arthur could not rid himself of a conception of naval strategy which Nelson would have found outdated. Three of the four Sea Lords went overboard. One of the new body of colleagues had to sleep in the Admiralty every fourth night to be at hand for an "unexpected" event that everyone was waiting for. In constituting his new Board of Admiralty, Churchill brushed aside four or five senior Admirals. Automatic promotion ceased; everywhere young officers were appointed to the most responsible commands. Jellicoe was entrusted with the rank of second-in-command of the Home Fleet. The older Admirals were near explosion. But no one remonstrated. Jellicoe was Jackie's first disciple.

And here the most fantastic character among all the great, extraordinary, and historic figures who had crossed Churchill's ways entered his life.

John Arbuthnot Lord Fisher (*Punch*)

JOHN ARBUTHNOT LORD FISHER and Winston Churchill had made a chance acquaintance in Biarritz, five years before. "Jackie," as Fisher was affectionately called, fell instantly under Winston's spell. Twice Churchill's age, Fisher flooded his friend with letters, beginning "Beloved Winston" and ending with "Yours till hell freezes." The old man could not express himself without the violence of a tornado. "May their wives be widows!" he cursed his opponents — all those who did not understand his great ideas. "May your children be fatherless and your home be a dunghill!" he said benevolently, when he dismissed a ranking admiral.

The Navy loved him. A year before Churchill's appointment the fire-eater had reached his seventieth year, retirement age. The Admiralty worked considerably more smoothly without him, even under Churchill, who wielded his iron broom with kid gloves. But after Jackie's resignation his desk remained unoccupied. No one would have committed the sacrilege of stepping into the old man's shoes.

The father of the Navy was the only expert whom Churchill wished as an adviser. He visited the veteran in Reigate Priory, his *buen retiro*. For hours the old friends exploded in unison, like two volcanoes. Churchill had to return to his office. Precipitately, the oldster accompanied him. At Waterloo Station they parted, Churchill with a bright smile and a respectful bow. Lord Fisher did not stretch out his hand. He nodded haughtily, and turned around. This son of a bastard had not spoken the word.

The father of the Navy was spoiling to return to his empty desk. Churchill had felt it during their whole conversation. But at this time of grave emergency he was not accessible to human considerations. It was impossible to let Fisher resume his old personal system of confusing and confounding the Admiralty. Churchill himself had all the necessary drive his mission needed. He wanted Fisher's advice, not his presence.

The old man sulked in his tent. Nevertheless, every day he wrote elaborate, irascible letters to the First Lord, full of practical wisdom and precious advice.

Mostly the First Lord accepted his advice. On one crucial occasion he did not. History has fully vindicated Churchill's refusal. But it caused the gravest setback in his whole career.

CIVIL HEAD OF THE ADMIRALTY: MR. WINSTON CHURCHILL AS FIRST
LORD. This photograph was taken during the political crisis. Mr. Winston Churchill became First Lord of the Admiralty in 1911, and in that
capacity, at the outbreak of the war, he earned great credit for his
promptitude in mobilizing the Fleet. He has also been Home Secretary, President of the Board of Trade, and Under-Secretary for the
Colonies.   (*Illustrated News*, London)

UNTIL this setback materialized, the new First Lord was generally, and rightly, regarded as a miracle worker. Dissatisfaction was rampant among the crews when Churchill assumed office. Pamphlets and magazines, edited and distributed quite openly by able seamen and retired mates, complained about bad conditions, harsh discipline, too low wages in the Navy. The "father of the Navy" had already done a good deal to ameliorate the sailors' standards, but grumbling went on.

Churchill wanted to have happy and efficient ships. He examined every grudge, and decided to clear up the mess. He abolished all unsocial conditions. Pittance wages were raised by 30 per cent. Humiliating bodily punishment was abrogated. Working hours were shortened. The Sunday off became more real. The most consequential innovation was Churchill's decision to open commissions to able seamen. Whenever the First Lord appeared, the lower decks cheered.

At the top Churchill instituted a Naval Staff, the brain trust of the Royal Navy, through which all candidates for naval command had to pass. It was, however, only an advisory body. The responsibility for decisions rested with the First Lord alone. Surrounded by his hand-picked councilors, he was the commander. For the first time since many years the First Lord was not the mouthpiece of the Sea Lords. A ranking statesman had arisen to confront Tirpitz.

His other preoccupation, next to purely naval matters, revealed his truly visionary sense. Churchill became the founder of the British air arm. His achievements in the Navy may, at that time, have appeared more conspicuous, but his prescience of the importance of the air as a theater of war remains one of his great, perhaps his greatest, contribution to England. When he took over the Admiralty the Royal Navy had about six airplanes and as many pilots. Everything else had to be created by Churchill, who was responsible for the development of the Royal Air Service for eleven years, with the exception of the year 1916. From 1911 to 1915 he nursed and expanded the air force as First Lord; to the end of the war as Minister of Munitions, responsible for production and supply; and from 1919 to 1921 as both Air Minister and Secretary for War. Incessantly he preached air power throughout the following years, in or out of office. When Hitler's shadow arose, long before he had become the Fuehrer, Churchill threw his full weight into his crusade. Under his war leadership the miracle of the R. A. F. came into being.

81

When he began this one-man campaign, even Mr. Punch, usually his faithful ally, was mildly derisive.

NEPTUNE'S ALLY.

(*The First Lord of the Admiralty calls in a new element to redress the balance of the old.*)

CHURCHILL established a Royal Flying Corps with naval and military sections in the school on Salisbury Plain. He himself became its first pupil. He had more air crashes during the first years of his solo flights than any other young pilot. Of course he flew more recklessly and with more daring than any other man. But then, he also had more escapes from death in battle than his fair share. Has Winston Churchill a charmed life? Providence, it appears, needs him on earth.

Churchill as a student pilot at the Salisbury Plain Flying School (*Punch*)

TOWARD the end of April, H. M. battleship *Hibernia* put to sea with four hydroplanes on board and special facilities to launch them. At the same time Churchill's reorganization of the Royal Navy was accomplished. Her active list now formed three great fleets. On May Day, 1912, King George V came as the First Lord's personal guest to review the great parade at Southampton.

The fleet had shifted from coal to oil fuel, thus tremendously increasing the ship's cruising radius. Oil was the new lifeblood of the Royal Navy. Lord Fisher agreed with this reform. He stopped sulking in his tent to accept the chairmanship of the oil-fuel commission. For a time his relation with Churchill was restored. It was again "Beloved Winston."

Mr. Punch notes Mr. Churchill's shifting of the Fleet from coal to oil fuel.

(*Punch*)

SUCH was his vision for the air force, such was his struggle for the navy. But he assumed a third task, entirely outside the scope of the Admiralty. Churchill was the Government's honest broker with the Irish Home Rulers. He had been deeply entrenched in the Irish struggle, but he saw plainly now that it was no longer the constitution or the loss of a rebellious province that was at stake, but the fate of the Empire. The First Lord introduced the

Second Home Rule Bill. It was none of his official business, but as ever, in an emergency, he acted. He did not want to give up Ulster. He realized that only the Orangemen's stubborn defiance could save Belfast from Dublin's tyranny. But at the same time the open preparations of the Ulstermen under Lord Londonderry for civil war annoyed him. With a war for the existence of the Empire inevitably approaching, he had no use for civil war, patriotic or not.

He accepted an invitation from the Belfast Liberals to address a meeting in Ulster Hall. The Captains of the Orangemen were in commotion. Lord Londonderry threatened that the meeting would simply not take place. But when the British Government sent troops into town to protect the right of free speech, at the cost of £2,730, Londonderry acquiesced to letting the meeting take place, if not in Ulster Hall, at least on a football ground, where a faithful multitude listened to Churchill's speech. Due to the great military summons, his every word cost the taxpayer 15 shillings.

THE MODERN SAMSON. Sending fire into the fields of the Philistines
(*Newcastle Weekly Chronicle*)

THE PROTECTOR. Lord Londonderry: "I only want to protect you!" Mr. Churchill and Mr. John Redmond: "It's very kind of you, but we're not 'Babes in the Wood,' and we aren't lost!"

(*Westminster Gazette*)

FOR the same reason Lord Londonderry declared that his armed Orange-men had only gathered to protect the speakers, Mr. Churchill and Mr. John Redmond.

CHURCHILL delivered a quiet, non-controversial speech, just to cool off the hot-tempered listeners. A soaking deluge of rain contributed a good deal toward achieving Churchill's purpose. But the greatest contribution to quelling a riot that never broke out, more than all the cavalry and infantry in town, was the presence of "Clemmie," standing next to her husband, and smiling brightly and cheerfully.

British troops arriving in Belfast to quell the riots that never occurred

A CABINET meeting late in July was entirely concerned with the Irish troubles. At the end of the session a messenger from the Foreign Office brought a sealed envelope to Sir Edward Grey, who silently opened it and handed it to the Premier. Quietly, Asquith read to his colleagues the Austrian ultimatum to Serbia.

Winston Churchill rushed back to his office. Instantly he published a communiqué, a final warning to Germany: "The Fleet is remaining at home positions." On July 27 he warned the commanders that hostilities might begin at any moment. On Tuesday, August 7, at eleven o'clock, his General Order went out to the Royal Navy: "Commence hostilities against Germany at once."

At midnight the great Kitchener opened the door of the First Lord's office. He stretched out his hand. He said: "There is one thing they cannot take away from you: 'The Fleet was ready!' "

Lord Kitchener as Secretary of War, at the outbreak of the First World War

Kladderadatch, Germany's leading satirical weekly, views Winston's
Battle with the U-Boats

THE superhuman nervous tension burst out in a stream of tears that
rolled down Churchill's cheeks, as Asquith announced to the House:
"Great Britain is at war!" Within five minutes, however, Winston had fully
recovered from three years of strain. His supreme duty was to conquer
the U-boat, which he recognized as the most perilous danger long before
Tirpitz had let his first squads loose.

89

Churchill leading British Marines through the streets of Antwerp

WITHIN the first few days of the war Churchill was generally regarded as the leader of the War Party in the cabinet. John Morley and Sir John Simon had already resigned to demonstrate their peace-at-any-price-mindedness. Churchill had no personal following in his own party, while the Conservatives still nursed their old grudges against him. Only the overwhelming popularity he had won by his stupendous mobilization of the Fleet supported him.

At the height of this tension, on September 28, 1914, the German bombardment of Antwerp began. Kitchener made a suggestion: "You must personally dash to Antwerp," he told Churchill, "and explain to Brouqueville that he must hold out with the help of the Royal Navy Division another four days, until British reenforcements arrive."

The suggestion was immediately accepted. The war cabinet counted on Winston's magic spell. He, if no one else, would keep the Belgian government in line. Churchill himself yearned for another good fight. He did not only explain his mission to Brouqueville. He assumed personal command of the contingent of British Marines. At the head of his troops he paraded through the streets of Antwerp to cheer up the entirely downhearted Belgians.

90

"Winston is more important in the center of things." Lord Asquith

THE Marines changed into battledress and took up position in the furthermost line. Again old General Ian Hamilton observed Churchill at work: "Winston handles them as if he were Napoleon and they the Old Guard. He flings them right into the enemy's open jaw."

The Marines were only 8,000 men. Their fiery spirit of attack, indeed, kindled the Belgian resistance for another four days. But no British re-enforcements arrived. The lost division, Churchill ahead, fought like lions. When their ammunition gave out, they drew their swords, and, brilliantly trained swordsmen as they were, stood another day against overwhelming German man- and firepower. No General Rawlinson yet with the promised thirty to forty thousand men. No supplies, no ammunition.

Churchill cabled his resignation as First Lord. He wanted to take over the Belgian Army, and make a desperate stand at Antwerp with their 130,000 surviving men. Kitchener, now entirely convinced of Winston's military genius, offered immediately to make him Lieutenant-General. Wise old Asquith shook his head. "Winston is more important in the center of things." He refused the First Lord's resignation, and called upon him to return to his desk with utmost speed. Churchill obeyed, convinced that Asquith was right. It was the last time in his life that he had followed his passion, instead of cool reflection.

THE U-boat peril increased. "Baby-killers!" Churchill exclaimed. The word caught the English imagination even more than Asquith's "Wait and see!" The First Lord promised: "We will dig them out of their rat holes!"

German cartoonists answer Winston's boast against the U-Boats

THE sinking of the *Lusitania* in May, 1915, was the first event during the first World War that brought home to American public opinion the proximity of the danger. Imperial Germany's propaganda strained every nerve to burden Churchill with the guilt for their own crime.

93

AT the end of October, Louis, Prince of Battenberg, retired on account of his German name which caused widespread misgivings. The post of First Sea Lord was free again. Churchill hastened to offer it to Lord Fisher, at seventy-four more vital and alert than ever. Next to Churchill, or perhaps even his peer, old man Jackie was the foremost naval brain in the world. His devotion to Winston, now he had recalled the "father of the Navy,"

Not at all downhearted at going to the Front: Mr. Winston Churchill leaving his home with Mrs. Churchill. He left London early on the morning of Thursday, November 18, for France, to join his regiment, the Queen's Own Oxfordshire Hussars, in which he was a major. Mrs. Churchill went to the station to see him off.

(*Photo by Illustrations Bureau*)

bordered on idolatry. Unfortunately the harmony between them could not last. The two headstrong men, so unequal in age, so similar in temperament, could simply not get along with one another. Gallipoli brought their separation.

At the peak of their fight both antagonists were ousted by a political coup. Secretly Mr. Asquith had agreed upon a coalition government with Mr. Bonar Law, the Conservative leader, whose party still did not want to have any dealings and doings with Churchill, the "renegade." Lord Fisher, for his part, demanded absolute authority over the naval war. He wanted to serve neither under Churchill nor under Bonar Law nor Mr. Balfour. His resignation was implied, and accepted. Churchill was paid off with the Duchy of Lancaster, a mere sinecure. "Four thousand pounds a year for doing nothing? In the midst of the war?" he laughed. He volunteered for front-line service.

Smilingly, he left his family and home.

Mr. Punch depicts Winston, the swashbuckler of old, reporting to Sir John French at Calais

Churchill as Colonel of the
Sixth Battalion of the Scotch
Fusiliers

AT forty-one he went to school again. He was appointed Major of the
Grenadier Guards, under instruction previous to higher appointment.
Again he heard the bullets whistle. Again he had a number of hairbreadth
escapes. Again, it proved, Providence had further use for him.

Among the many distinguished visitors he received was Lord Birken-head, a Conservative, nevertheless a faithful friend of Churchill. "We want you back in the center of events," he said. "All want you back. . . . Remember, the Naval Estimates will come up in a few days!"

The temptation was irresistible. On the other hand, he hated to leave his battalion. He had been a father to every man, and they in turn adored him. He hesitated. Birkenhead, a spellbinder if there ever was one, conjured up the magic of the House, the goal of all striving. Churchill could not resist. He was really more important in the House. He bade farewell to his Grenadiers. He noted every man's name and, after demobilization, he saw to it that each found a decent job.

The House cheered the prodigal son's return. Even his most violent opponents had missed him. He, too, was far above revengefulness. His first speech pointed out the increasing danger of the U-boat. "There was a time when I did not think I could have brought myself to say it. But I have been away for some months, and my mind is now clear. My advice is to recall Lord Fisher."

Lloyd George listened to his speech with visible attention, which was a rare event, since he preferred to have others listen to him. England needed Winston's voice. When the Welshman formed his own government, he simply must have Churchill in it. Asquith, Lloyd George, and Winston Churchill were good friends, and politically closely associated. But each, in turn, was eleven years younger than the other — and that decided.

After his first speech Churchill returned to the furthermost front line. Asquith had obviously no opening for him. Besides, Churchill himself would not have accepted one. After seven months of combat service, he like every front-line soldier, was through with the senile and ever-undecided Premier.

Churchill was appointed Colonel of the 6th battalion of the Scotch Fusiliers. The losses of British troops in the Battle of the Somme were so terrible that battalions had to be fused. The Commander of the 7th battalion, Winston's senior in rank, took over Churchill's men, too.

AT the same time Mr. Asquith's Premiership had become untenable. The lingering political crisis came into the open. A torrent of voices from England demanded Churchill, a colonel without a battalion, back. Lloyd George pressed him.

Gravely, Churchill pondered his position. Had he not done enough already to seek a hero's death? Was it not really senseless to control a minute portion of the fighting line? He returned to the House. There he pressed immediately for the increase and expansion of military aviation. If Britannia did not also rule the clouds, one day she would no longer rule the waves either.

Churchill as Minister of Munitions (*Photo by C. Vandyke*)

In December, 1916, Lloyd George formed his cabinet to win the war. It took him a few months to persuade the last grumblers that Churchill was the necessary man. He was still a dangerous man, too. The Conservatives wanted nothing of him.

Two months later Lloyd George had overcome all objection and could make Churchill Minister of Munitions. Winston had a new lease on life. America had joined the Allies. British war production rose by leaps and bounds, since the American Government had entrusted Mr. Churchill with the immense commission of equipping its growing army in France.

Hilarity of Mr. Churchill on hearing his chief's views about Russia.   (*Punch*)

UNTIL the end of the war, Churchill slept in his Ministry and spent his days alternately in his office and in flying visits to the front in France. Then came the day when all bells were ringing. Winston Churchill, his wife at his side, rode through Whitehall. When they turned the corner into Downing Street, Lloyd George stood there waiting. With a silent handshake the two war leaders celebrated peace.

Aggressive, imperialist Germany was shattered. But Churchill saw a new ruthless and threatening tyranny arising: the terror of Bolshevism. At that time the Big Five, the Allies, were still giving lukewarm and half-hearted support to the White Russian generals. Churchill was accused of pressing for all-out assistance. In fact, he did nothing more than carry out strictly the decisions of the Supreme Council in Paris, and of his own government. The whole British contribution to the White Russian generals was less than fifty millions. Lloyd George, however, did not care for the whole business. In Paris his was the chief influence to give up the help to Denikin, whose troops were still in the field. In London he had a serious talk with Winston, asking him to desist from his anti-bolshevist tirades. Churchill had to yield – to his great displeasure.

99

AFTER the Khaki Election in December, 1918, Churchill advanced further in the government hierarchy. He became War Minister and Air Secretary at once. Captain Wedgwood Benn, a persistent gadfly, mocked: "In his youth Winston was a medal-snatcher and self-advertiser; now he is a portfolio collector." Churchill gave one of his at once massive and subtle replies. Mr. Punch expressed it:

THE TANK AND THE LITTLE BRICK. (Mr. Churchill and Captain Wedgwood Benn) "The tank, weighing thirty tons, is able to pass over a brick lying on the road without crushing it. This is a very important point." Mr. Churchill.   (Punch)

Churchill reviews the Women's Auxiliaries in the Stadtwaeldchen,
Cologne. (*Sphere*)

AS War Minister in the demobilization days, he worked another of the
already proverbial "Winston miracles." Millions of British soldiers were
streaming home from all the corners of the globe. Within less than six
months every man had his job, and was reintegrated in civilian society.

Churchill's martial office also had its more pleasant aspects. He visited
the British contingents, occupying the Rhineland, and cast a friendly
glance at the Women's Auxiliaries, gathered in parade in the Stadtwaeldchen, Cologne.

Mr. Winston Churchill (returning from the Rhine): "What! No official motorcar? Well, this brings the peace home to one." (*Punch*)

ON his return from the Rhineland no official car was waiting at Victoria Station. This, of course, was an oversight. But the war lord felt it a blessing: peace!

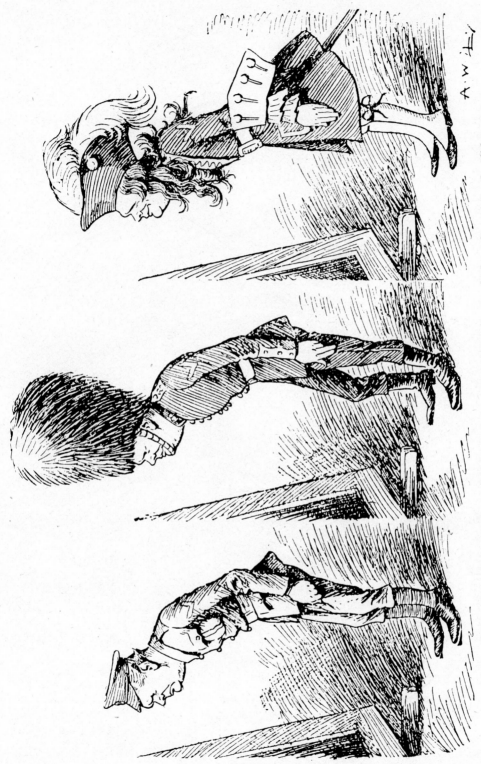

Mr. Churchill Sees Red. Army uniform (1) as it is; (2) as it was before the war and will be again; and (3) as, to suit Mr. Churchill's Marlborough traditions, it should have been

(*Punch*)

A "Futurist" Landscape. Mr. Churchill gets busy (*Punch*)

IN the spring of 1921 Churchill moved to the Colonial Office where he had
held his first office as Under-Secretary sixteen years before, while retain-
ing the Air Ministry. A strong hand was required to bring order into the
Colonial administration. It had just been necessary to suppress a very
bloody revolution in Iraq. The running feud between Arabs and Jews
threatened to explode at any moment. The whole Middle East was in a
desperate condition.

He held a conference in Cairo, at which, next to a selected circle of ad-
ministrators, even Lawrence of Arabia participated. Lawrence was known
as the most difficult man on earth, but he got along with Churchill very
well. In the *Seven Pillars of Wisdom* he paid the Colonial Minister the
following tribute: "Churchill in a few weeks made straight all the tangles,
finding solutions, fulfilling, I think, our promises in spirit and letter, where
humanly possible, without sacrificing any interest of the Empire or of the
people concerned."

Mr. Punch views Mr. Churchill's hobby of painting (*Punch*)

TO play down the importance of the conference, Churchill ostensibly enjoyed his favorite hobby, painting. This time he painted the Pyramids — while Lloyd George reshuffled his cabinet once more, in order to win stronger Conservative support. Everyone expected that Winston Churchill would be asked to take the post of the Chancellor of the Exchequer: the most successful member of many Ministries, England's most popular statesman, and still the United Kingdom's knight in white armor, had full claim to it.

Mr. Winston Churchill (on his dahabeah): "Awfully rough on poor David in these trying times that I should have been 'taken away in the interest of the State.'" (*Punch*)

BUT absentees are always wrong. The Tory leadership stubbornly declared that the interest of the State forbade Churchill's appointment to the second-in-rank. Partly their old resentment was still lingering on, partly they feared that the Liberals would be too powerful in the coalition, if they held both leading posts. Churchill took it in his stride.

Winston as paternal adviser to the Prince of Wales

HAPPY days were here again. The Churchills mingled with society. Winston, slowly assuming the role of the heavy father, became paternal adviser to the Prince of Wales, later King Edward VII.

Stage manager of Coalition Company: "Quite a nice little scrap. One might almost think you were almost fighting." Sir A., Griffith—Boscawem, Mr. Churchill, Mr. Lloyd George   (*Punch*)

LLOYD GEORGE was not pleased. He still relished, with a bystander's smile, minor frictions between Liberal and Conservative members of his coalition cabinet, in which his stormy petrel was invariably involved. But he felt forebodings.

Churchill carried to train after appendicitis operation (*Sphere*)

IT did not remain minor friction between Lloyd George's younger colleagues. His own leadership was attacked by the die-hards, who were getting weary of playing second fiddle. On Sunday, October 22, 1921, Churchill gave a reconciliation dinner at his house. Curzon, Birkenhead, Austen Chamberlain, Lloyd George, and the landlord pledged in solemn toasts and after-dinner speeches that they would hold together. On Tuesday Churchill spoke in Bristol, announcing to the country that the rumors of a government crisis were unfounded. On Thursday Viscount Curzon did not appear in the Carlton Club. This was, in the most gentlemanlike manner, an unmistakable indication that he would no longer support the Government. Its Tory members resigned. Lloyd George was deprived of a majority. He fell, dragging down the hero of the session.

The ensuing general elections returned a slight majority of Tories. The true outcome, however, was a Red landslide. The Liberals almost disappeared. Churchill suffered an attack of appendicitis. He was operated on. Three days later, still barely able to talk, he dictated a message to his voters in Dundee. Mrs. Churchill conveyed the message. Supported by a few friends, she tirelessly campaigned for her bedridden husband. But Winston shocked his doctor by insisting on being carried to the train for Dundee.

A RIOTOUS mob of newly enfranchised voters received him with a howl. Dundee was teeming with Socialists and Communists. Churchill was beaten by 10,000 votes. For the first time since 1900 he was out of the House.

He had long learned to take philosophically the ups and downs of fate.

Winston takes an early morning walk on the lawn
at Chartwell   (*Sphere*)

True, his prophetic voice would now be dimmed, since in England out of Parliament means out of public life. He was excluded, just now when the country was entering a grave internal crisis. He pondered his own case.

Winston examining the morning mail in his Chartwell study. (*Sphere*)

Chartwell Manor, the Churchill country home, three-quarters of an hour away from Whitehall. (*Sphere*)

Churchill in the room where histories have been written and naval campaigns against the Nazis planned   (*Sphere*)

At the last election he was returned by 20,000 votes; this time he was beaten by 10,000. Those who had shifted represented the politically floating population. If his was a test case, England would go down in self-deception and weakness.

Still an invalid, Mr. Churchill retired to his villa in Cannes for six months of complete rest. He spent his vacation by pacing up and down his room with rapid steps from breakfast to lunch, dictating what was to become (at least until his book about the second World War) his masterwork, *The World Crisis,* an account of the first war and its origins. The first volume appeared in April, 1923; the next on October 2. The author was not yet quite fifty years old. Yet he was already recognized as one of the greatest writers in English prose and the foremost historian of our time. Besides, he was an elder statesman for whom his nation had not much use.

After six months on the Côte d'Azur, the Churchills moved home to Chartwell Manor, the beautiful old house three miles from Westerham, Kent. It was intended to be his last abode. Mr. Churchill called it his home for the "duration." (Few people realize that this much-used term, like a great many other household words, was coined by Churchill.) Gradually he turned into the country squire, whose image became familiar to, and was beloved by, all England.

The Churchills at home (*Sphere*)

Churchill as bricklayer. He belongs to the union. (*Strand*)

HIS poor health forced him to give up sports. He replaced them with brick-laying. But the bricklayers protested against a non-union member working at Chartwell Manor. Churchill filled out a card for the bricklayers' union, and applied for membership.

The cartoonists attack Churchill for inconsistency.

IN December, 1923, Mr. Stanley Baldwin followed his fellow conservative, Bonar Law, as Prime Minister. Obviously to distract the people's minds from the incipient German rearmament, he brought forward another issue that would excite the English people even more. He suddenly reopened the Protectionist issue. But the people rejected high tariffs. In droves the voters shifted to the Socialists, who did not win a majority at new elections, but were helped into the saddle by the residue of Asquith's Liberals.

Churchill considered this election the height of insanity. Prophetically he foresaw that the moderate parties would break each other's heads again. The Socialists alone would profit. Nevertheless, he could not keep silent in the face of another attack of Protectionism. A great many constituencies offered him their candidacy. He chose the most difficult job, the radical district of West Leicester, and was promptly beaten by Mr. Pethick-Lawrence, a recent convert to Socialism.

Mr. Asquith, now a spiteful old man with nothing left of the statesman-philosopher, was still brooding over the Conservative-Lloyd George conspiracy. He wanted no dealings and doings with the Tories, and hence sacrificed his own last platoon of followers to support the MacDonald minority. Twenty years after Churchill had crossed the floor with the words, "Thank God that we have a Liberal Party!" he quit it. It was the death blow. For all practical purposes England had no more Liberal Party since Churchill had left it in disgust.

Once more, as in his youth, he was accused of "inconsistency." He answered with a smile: "Who is inconsistent? I? Because England stands above parties to me? I am the most consistent of all!"

He fought for a lost cause. But thousands all over the British Isles worshiped him.

Winston weathers the storm

MR. CHURCHILL was not yet back in the Conservative fold. He called himself a "Constitutionalist." The word sounded makeshift, and was much derided. But it did, indeed, express his creed. England's constitution, even if unwritten, is the lasting value. Churchill had outgrown ephemeral interests. Right, Left, progress, and reaction became empty words to him. He was only concerned with the lasting, the essential thing, the balance, harmony, and eternity of England. "Constitutionalist" came near to expressing this faith.

He was weary of politics. But the signs of the times horrified him. The Fascist rabble in Italy, the Reichswehr building the "secret" airdromes in Russia, the beer-cellar harangues of Hitler — all these disturbing events were not isolated incidents. To Churchill it was the expression of nations with will power. England must match this will power, and best it. And so Winston Churchill came out of self-chosen retirement in his country

117

house. As an independent candidate, he stood for a by-election in the Abbey Division of Westminster, an English miniature Washington, including Buckingham Palace, both Houses of Parliament, the seat of government, the principal theaters, clubs, St. James's Street, and the Strand, but also the slums of Soho. Cabinet members, the theatrical crowd, important personages vote here, but also the rowdies of Soho.

The by-election in this small district, in February, 1924, became the most talked-of political event in years. The official Conservative candidate beat Winston Churchill by forty votes out of some twenty thousand. It was his third defeat in a row. But all the independent minds in the Conservative Party had supported him. Thirty Tory M. P.'s exposed themselves to the danger of being excluded from the party and themselves losing their seats, in campaigning for Churchill. The Young Conservatives arrived in serried ranks to vote for "daddy Winston." *Grandess dames*, duchesses and ladies of the peerage, canvassed for Churchill. But so did the chorus girls from the theatrical district. The musicians, the prize fighters, the jockeys, and other popular favorites came out vigorously for their champion.

On the other side the rowdies of Soho, a good number of them foreigners, staged a riotous anti-Churchill demonstration on behalf of comrade Fenner-Brockway, their Socialist candidate. Strangely enough, the police did nothing to quell these riots, though every bobby adored his one-time chief. Scotland Yard had another opportunity to be grateful to Churchill. In the demonstration against him, the Yard could pick out a respectable quantity of long-sought-after underworld characters.

Churchill's triumphal defeat was a demonstration of England's desire for fair play. Mr. Baldwin could no longer disregard him. The very day after the decision of Westminster he offered the moral victor a safe Conservative seat in Epping, the one the Prime Minister holds to this day. Mr. and Mrs. Churchill betook themselves to Epping.

Churchill as Chancellor
of the Exchequer

CHURCHILL returned as a full-fledged Conservative member. Very soon Mr. Baldwin made him Chancellor of the Exchequer. Now Winston reached his life-long aim. He could begin where his father had been fated to end.

119

The Chancellorship made the Churchills smile

AMONG other hereditary traits, Winston had also inherited Lord Randolph's supreme contempt for small sums. Both were retrenchers only to capitalize on their popularity with the lower income brackets. But in their private conception, money began with millions. Anything beneath six-digit figures was "decimals" to Winston.

How would this cavalier — more than once in his lifetime an impecunious cavalier — fit into the Treasury, England's Holy Grail, where heaps of minute decimals were piled upon each other, to keep the United Kingdom a going concern?

To general astonishment, the new Chancellor was perfectly fit for his new surroundings. All-round genius can grasp any problem it has to face. Moreover, Churchill had, in his radical and critical years, himself been a keen budget critic, mastering the minutest detail of England's ledger. Finally, in the reparation discussions at Paris, where he now assisted as the United Kingdom's chief delegate, he was surrounded by the world's outstanding financiers. It was an excellent finishing school. Speedily Winston grasped the more mysterious tricks of the trade. Unfortunately, his old problem faced him once more: the talk was about millions, even billions, and the result — German reparation payments — decimals, indeed.

He was now nearer the center of things than ever in his previous career. True, he had outgrown personal ambitions. Yet there was a "je ne sais quoi" to the Chancellorship that made the happy Churchills smile.

Mr. Winston Churchill takes his wife and children to the House of Commons to hear his budget speech

HIS first budget was a most moderate "poor man's" budget. Death duties were increased, a duty was imposed on silk. The McKenna duties on motor-cars and pianos were revived, which caused Mr. Punch to remark:

THE MCKENNA DUTIES. Mr. Churchill rehearses a retrospective attitude   (*Punch*)

"PULL PHILIP, PULL DAVID." Master Winston (the King of the Castle):
"So long as they tug at me from opposite directions I feel pretty safe."
(In the debate on the Finance Bill the Chancellor of the Exchequer
described the criticisms directed against his Budget as "unrelated, con-
tradictory, and mutually destructive.") (*Punch*)

FURTHERMORE, the budget included the return to the gold standard.
This was not Mr. Churchill's own idea. He had, in fact, accepted the sug-
gestions of an expert committee set up under the previous government.
Nevertheless, the measure aroused irate opposition against the Chancellor,
with Lloyd George and Philip Snowden as chief noisemakers. Each proposed amendments contrary to those of his fellow critic. Only in their
malice against Churchill were they of one mind. Lloyd George was out of
power for good, and he knew it. But the aged man's temper was just as hot
as it had been in his youth. Although Mr. Churchill remains courteous to
his former chief up to this day, Lloyd George could never forgive that
Winston was ever growing, whereas David, himself, was gradually fading.

Also the maniac spite of Philip Snowden was a case of jealousy. The
later Viscount Snowden was widely regarded as the financial Pope of
Socialism. Indeed, he had a penetrating mind and an extraordinary gift
for fault-finding, and for slashing attacks.

Churchill remained unmoved. He relished the impotent rage from both
sides.

LOWER HOUSE COMEDY. Mr. Winston Churchill on
Unemployment Insurance   (*Punch*)

MR. CHURCHILL'S second budget was again highly controversial. He
imposed a tax on betting, the hallowed pastime of king and beggar. The
Conservatives duly passed the measure, though silently and in an embarrassed mood. To most of the Tory members it was a slashing self-
imposed tax. Liberals and Socialists roared that the Chancellor was taking
away the poor man's only pleasure in life. Whereupon Churchill outdid
their professional social feelings: "I need the betting tax to make possible
the increase of unemployment insurance."

Phil and Win, the famous back-chat comedians. Every-other-daily performances

(*Punch*)

FOR the rest of his tenure of the Treasury Mr. Churchill was engaged in his running feud with Snowden. In day sessions they fought with a truly English pre-war weapon.

AN ALL-NIGHT ENTERTAINMENT. Mr. Snowden and Mr. Churchill remain at grips.

(*Punch*)

DURING night sessions, however, when tempers get hot, the duel became a wrestling match.

A Knock-About Mimic; or, Going the Whole Hod. Mr. Churchill: "Very Flattering!" *(Punch)*

WITH the exception of the General Strike in 1926, which led England to the brink of disaster until it was crushed by the resolute citizens under Churchill's vigorous guidance, his further conduct in the Treasury was uncontested. It looked as if he would remain Chancellor for life.

But at the General Elections of 1929 Mr. Ramsay MacDonald, long past his revolutionary start, in fact irresistibly attracted by the glamour of old England, staged a comeback. The Conservatives, with Churchill, resigned, without any grudge against MacDonald. In addition, the ex-chancellor had the pleasure of watching Mr. Snowden, his successor in the Treasury, adopting and copying all the measures he himself had introduced.

127

With the smile of a tiger, Mr. Churchill, together with three of his
retired colleagues, return for the last time in a gilded state-coach from
their audience with the King   (*Sphere*)

GRADUALLY Churchill became the sage. With an outlook far ahead of
his generation, he had always been a visionary. But now he retired into the
past. For ten years already he had devoted most of his free time to writing
the biography of the Duke of Marlborough, his ancestor. Now, unwanted
by a nation stricken with sleeping sickness, he sought comfort in the days
of England's greatness. He did not in the least believe that these days were
gone. "It may well be that the most glorious chapters in our history are
yet to be written," he said in addressing the Royal Society of St. George.
But the dreary interval between two great periods was unbearable.
The Life of Marlborough, in four heavy tomes, full of fight, was again a
classic historiography. It is certainly one of the greatest escape stories in
world literature.

With the book done, and enthusiastically received, Churchill went to
America. First, for painting, to the Canadian Rockies; then, embarking
on a lecture tour, to the United States. On the evening before his first
announced appearance on the platform, he was about to visit Mr. Baruch.
As Churchill crossed Fifth Avenue a taxi knocked him down. Churchill
had forgotten that traffic in America was the other way of the road.

THE SELF-CHUKKER. Mr. Churchill has retired from the Business
Committee of the Conservative Party. (Rare piece of the Mogul
School, 18th Century)   (*Punch*)

SOON after his return to England, in the first days of February, 1931, Mr.
Churchill retired from the Business Committee of the Conservative Party.
The whole country was impressed by his proud and magnificent attitude
of personal isolation. Like a temperamental but extremely skillful polo
player, he was suddenly weary of his mediocre team. He decided to go
away and have a game all by himself. That was Winston.

Churchill as Cassandra

HIS weariness was fully vindicated when, on August 25, the first so-called "National Government," the cabinet in which Messrs. MacDonald and Baldwin shared power, began its work. Now began the policy of appeasement with a vengeance. Japan seized Mukden on September 18, and established the Manchurian puppet state on February 15, 1932. This was the first and last time that America, otherwise deeply steeped in her "hands-off-the-world!" policy, was willing to take joint action. But Sir John Simon, then English Foreign Secretary, refused any practical steps. By a small minority the Germans elected Hindenburg, not Hitler, Reichspresident. Thus the danger of Nazism seemed completely quelled. London put pressure on Paris to disarm immediately, since the English sense of fair play could no longer grant less than equality of armament to a Germany that had again decided for the pacifist Hindenburg, the man of granite with a golden heart.

The old fighting cock could simply not stomach such a provocation of all good sense. He emerged from his idyll at Chartwell Manor, and delivered the first of his Cassandra speeches. Disregarding a bad attack of toothache, he thundered against the government policy, displayed a careworn, skeptical expression, and closed with the question: "Germany and France on equal terms in fighting? Do you want war?"

Churchill as Cassandra

THE FAT BOY OF EPPING. Mr. Winston Churchill
does his best to make our flesh creep   (*Punch*)

"BRITAIN'S hour of weakness is Europe's hour of danger!" he cried to the
House. No echo came. The Treasury Bench was half empty. Mr. MacDonald, his head deeply bent, was having a little nap. Mr. Baldwin gazed without expression into space. Foreign Secretary Sir John Simon was con-
spicuously absent. Churchill was only a second-string speaker. He spoke
for no party. Even his old friend Mr. Punch lifted his finger in gentle
warning.

THE CANNIBAL'S DAILY DIET. I-Geneva Broth. Mr. Ramsay MacDonald,
Sir John Simon, and Mr. Winston Churchill   (*Punch*)

NOW it was evident to those full of unctuous rectitude that Churchill was
the troublemaker, not Germany. But he persisted. Although he had once
been a staunch advocate of the League, he would not remain silent while
Geneva became a sounding board for defeatists.

133

THE MANIKIN AND THE SUPERMAN; OR, "IF I WERE DOING IT."
(After an engraving entitled "Malbrook." Bibliothèque Na-
tionale, Paris). Sir Thomas Inskip and Mr. Winston Churchill
(*Punch*)

HITLER came into power. The Reichstag went up in flames. During the
first week of the Nazi regime 500,000 people were thrown into the German
concentration camps that suddenly sprang up. Provocatively, the Luftwaffe paraded along Germany's western border and North Sea coast. In
England the estimates for the R.A.F. were reduced by £450,000. That
was what Sir Thomas Inskip called a Defence Program.

A CASTLE IN SPAIN. "Alas, it is only a daydream!" (*Punch*)

LORD Londonderry, who was soon to acquire world-wide fame as leader of the English Naziphiles, was Secretary of Air. In Geneva he proposed arbitration: all the great powers should reduce their aircraft to England's level, then the fifth contestant in the race, whereafter a further general cut of 33 per cent should follow. His Lordship called it an effort at arbitration. Mr. Churchill puffed his heaviest cigar. A dark cloud of blue smoke evaporated, engulfing the phantasmagoria of arbitration with the devil.

HITTING OUT. Mr. Churchill opens the season by scoring heavily in his most aggressive style. Inset: The ball. (Sir Stafford Cripps)
(*Punch*)

DEFEATISM makes strange bedfellows. Lord Londonderry, the "Ulster Fascist," was the red rag to the Socialists.

At that time Sir Stafford Cripps was the coldest thinker and debater in the House, but the hottest Socialist, standing left of Labor. He most eloquently shared the die-hard's desire for appeasement at any price. Since the cricket season was just opening. . . .

THE LIGHT OF EPPING. (left) As Mr. Winston Churchill thinks it ought to be, and (right) as it is. *(Punch)*

ON March 15, MacDonald, with the inevitable Sir John Simon, betook himself to Rome. Two days after their arrival Mussolini proposed the Four Power Pact. The League of Nations should be superseded, or even replaced, by Europe's Big Four. It was the dress rehearsal for Munich. Mr. MacDonald, back in London, sang the praises of this Pact, although it would imply the sharing of power in Europe by two democratic states and two dictatorships.

The lonely Churchill was the only man in Westminster who immediately grasped how rightly the French would feel betrayed if Hitler should close in on them with Italian support and English acquiescence. Once again he rose in warning: "As yet the Nazis have no other outlet than upon the Germans." The two decisive words were: *as yet*. Churchill had long understood that Nazism was not a domestic affair, not a European problem, but the aggressive greed for world domination. But he stood all alone. Even the BBC was denied to him.

"Le Lord Churchill embodied *le sang froid Anglais.*" (*L'Illustration*)

OUT of power, without office, spokesman for himself and for common sense, he strained every nerve to revive the *entente cordiale*. While his own people proceeded on their fatal way of deliberate blindness, the French admired his single-handed struggle. Still more they marveled at his quiet composure and smiling charm during his days of trial and tribulation. Indeed, le Lord Churchill embodied *le sang froid Anglais*.

Mr. Winston Churchill in conversation with Sir Assheton Pownall
at the Anglo-French Luncheon Club

PREMIER Chautemps came to London to visit him. The Anglo-French
Luncheon Club made Churchill an honorary member, whereas a leading
Swiss newspaper, one of the most influential in Europe, accused
MacDonald of deliberately endeavoring to weaken France.

139

Churchill before the Second World War

ON July 30, 1934, Churchill informed the House of Germany's secret air armaments, documented with information which he had painstakingly collected. Since the whole world already regarded him as the center of resistance against the spread of Nazism, unceasing streams of information from all countries poured into Chartwell Manor. He stressed four points. First, in spite of Versailles, Germany had already created a military air force, for the time being two-thirds as strong as the British. Second, by the end of 1935 her air force would be equal to the British. Third, some time in 1936 Germany would have supremacy in the air. Fourth, once Germany had the lead, Britain would perhaps never be able to overtake her.

A few months later this confidential information was confirmed by Hitler himself. Bent on a new attempt at appeasement, Sir John Simon visited the Fuehrer. Hitler admitted bluntly that his Luftwaffe had already outdone the R. A. F., and that his lead would increase day by day.

Now England knew exactly how long she would remain a happy island: two years, or three, at best. But only five of six hundred honorable members supported him, when Churchill moved in the House, in reply to the Address, the amendment: "But humbly represent to Your Majesty that, in the present circumstances of the world, the strength of our national defences, and especially of our air defenses, is no longer adequate to secure the peace, safety, and freedom of Your Majesty's faithful subjects."

Appeasement's enemy

TWO more years of listless appeasement lingered on, and of Churchill's desperate near solitude in the House. The cabinet reconstruction on June 8, 1935, with Baldwin taking back Premiership and MacDonald becoming Lord-President, made matters only worse. The reorganized Government immediately signed an Anglo-German Naval Agreement, condoning, and even praising, Germany's breach of the naval clauses of Versailles.

Churchill inspects new tanks as he prepares, personally, for war. (*Sphere*)

IN the first days of December, 1936, Mussolini's raid on Abyssinia; his defiance of the League of Nations; Baldwin's promise, "no great armament in this country," which had won him the November, 1935, election; Churchill's constant warnings, documented with facts and figures of Germany's high-speed armament and of the Nazi Fifth Column flooding all Europe — all this was suddenly forgotten. In August, 1936, Mrs. Wallis Simpson had come into the open. After October the Abdication crisis was publicly discussed.

On Monday, December 7, the House of Commons fluttered in excitement. At question time the Chamber was packed to the limit. Old Colonel Wedgwood, a veteran from the Boer War, inveterate Socialist, pottery millionaire, and a staunch subject of the King, asked for an early opportunity to discuss his motion affirming unalterable allegiance to His Majesty. "No, sir!" Baldwin answered. When Wedgwood wanted to continue, he was shouted down from all sides. The Speaker ruled him out. Mr. Baldwin declared "the question" had first been raised by the King himself, to whom the Government had tendered no advice "except on the subject of a morganatic marriage." He concluded in expressing the deep sympathy of the House for His Majesty.

Everyone expected Churchill to rise next. He was known for his intimate personal relations with the King, and since "the question" was entirely unrelated to Nazism, the whole House was eager to hear him.

Mr. Churchill was at Fort Belvedere, the historic royal forest retreat, where the King spent the week preceding the outbreak of the crisis and the three sad days that followed. Almost the whole time his chief adviser had kept him company, while Mr. Walter Monckton, Attorney-General to the Duchy of Cornwall, the chief negotiator between the King and the Premier, commuted between No. 10 and Fort Belvedere. Lord Louis Mountbatten's limousine had been seen once or twice at the gates of the Royal Manor.

Now Churchill and Mr. Monckton raced to Westminster, both silent and brooding over "the question." The session was still going on. Winston wanted to throw his power into the balance.

Churchill and Walter Monckton en route to Westminster   (*Sphere*)

A Hornet's Nest. Poor Winnie-the-Pooh! (*Punch*)

BUT when he entered the House, the honorable members had already made up their minds. Poor, innocent Colonel Wedgwood's gallant charge had only helped to consolidate the majority behind Baldwin, who was on the brink of retirement age, and whose personal stake in "the question" was whether he would retire as a king-maker or as a complete failure.

Churchill had the ear of the House. But as soon as he implored the honorable members that no irrevocable step should be taken without full information of Parliament, his colleagues made it painfully clear that his intervention was ill-timed. A disrespectful roar of "Sit down!" tried to stifle him. As soon as Winston raised his voice in reply, the Speaker interrupted with a motion of silence. At this the old servant of the House was instantly mute.

Turbulence among the faithful Commons continued for a while. Winston had a particular gift for starting up ——

"SANDSTORM"

FLOGGING A DEAD HORSE. "We are told that the House and still more of the country are sick and tired of this matter (Ministerial cheers)." Mr. Churchill. (*Punch*)

HE returned to Fort Belvedere, remained as a house guest for three days, the first and second still full of conferences and negotiations, the third secluded in his room, where he wrote a broadcast. On the evening of December 10, 1936, listeners around the globe heard, with deep emotion, the words of the abdicating King . . ."the woman I love. . . ."

Mr. Baldwin was created Earl Baldwin of Bewdley on May 28, 1937, and resigned on the same day. Mr. Neville Chamberlain became his successor. His merits are still disputed. But no one who knew him can deny that he was an introvert. Nature had made him the very opposite of Winston Churchill, the extrovert of them all.

Neville Chamberlain could hardly disguise his aversion against that man with the voice. Churchill, for his part, was long beyond and above personal feuds. His temperament exploded only once. Captain Duncan Sandys, M. P., husband of Churchill's oldest daughter Sarah, had more than a year earlier delivered a speech to the House which was attacked as divulging military secrets. An investigation proved this accusation completely unfounded.

A year afterward an overzealous adherent of Mr. Chamberlain brought up the matter once more.

Father-in-law Churchill exploded.

Even the Ministerialists cheered him. Neville Chamberlain apologized. He was all for fair play.

In Wellington's Boots (*Punch*)

NEVILLE CHAMBERLAIN was equally for fair play for Hitler. On September 28, 1938, he signed the Pact of Munich. Parliament greeted him with a triumphal demonstration.

Only the fools and the hypocrites did not understand that the Pact of Munich opened the road to war. War meant Churchill in power. Winston maintained that war was already on. True, the fight was still in the bloodless stage, as in Wellington's Portuguese days.

146

"Winnie is Back!"

AFTER Munich, Winston Churchill bided his time in Chartwell Manor. A hurricane of public opinion demanded his return to Westminster. But Churchill's time for talk had passed. He took part in no discussions, not even in international controversy.

On September 3, 1939, at the same time that Mr. Chamberlain made his solemn declaration of war, the wireless electrified all British crews on the seven seas with the happy news: "Winnie is back!"

He returned to his old desk, where he had first won world fame, this time in his favorite uniform of an Elder Brother of Trinity House.

147

Part Three

THE WAR LORD

Kladderadatsch of Berlin pictures Mr. Churchill as
poison-monger

THE German attack began, a few hours after the declaration of war, with
the sinking of the *Athenia,* a merchantman carrying mostly American and
English women and children to what they hoped would be the safety of
the other shores. The Admiralty issued an indignant communiqué, pointing
out that it was the case of the *Lusitania* all over again. Churchill's appeal to
American public opinion was unmistakable.

Kladderadatsch of Berlin, the foulest "satirical" weekly in the world,
replied with a cartoon of Churchill as a poison-monger. One of the syringes
on his table was inscribed *Athenia.*

"It was for Hitler to say when the war would begin. . . ." Churchill, October 1, 1939.

HITLER was always in the habit of concentrating his whole slander and vilification barrage upon one living target at a time. Once the archenemy of mankind was Stalin, later Dr. Benes, afterward Schuschnigg. From the very start of the war, up to this day, Mr. Churchill has been singled out. Once more Hitler vindicated his much vaunted "intuition." History has long recognized that the Fuehrer foundered on the rock that is Winston Churchill.

The First Lord gave a timely warning. In the first of his stirring wartime speeches, delivered on October 1, 1939, Churchill declared: "It was for Hitler to say when the war would begin. But it is not for him, or his successors, to say when it will end."

150

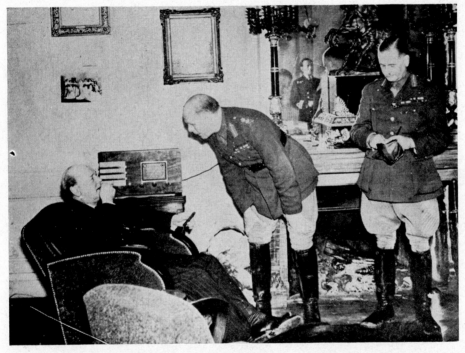

At British Headquarters in France with Viscount Gort and (right)
Lieutenant-General Pownall   (*British Official Photo*)

HIS man-killing job in the Admiralty left Mr. Churchill still time to look
after the British Expeditionary Force in France, and make an effort to
bolster French morale. He had some off-the-record talks in Paris. Then
he visited British headquarters. Here, in the drawing room of a French
château, a cozy log fire burning in the grate, he discussed the situation
with Viscount Gort, while Lieutenant-General Pownall listened in, and
filled his pipe.

151

"The First Lord spent his birthday with work as usual." (Communique).
Mr. Punch interprets the First Lord's "business as usual."   (*Punch*)

WINSTON'S NEW HAT (*Punch*)

THE full fury of the German air pirates, and their full load of bombs, were concentrated on Westminster, the heart of the city. Buckingham Palace and Westminster Abbey were hit. The savages were determined to destroy the three symbols of the British Empire, standing for the Throne, Christianity, and Democracy. The full terror of air power was still to come, and when it came, it struck the other way. But the blitz on England in 1940 was the peak of *schrecklichkeit* (frightfulness) in two thousand years of Teuton savagery.

Churchill termed this terrible time "our finest days," those he had predicted in his address to the Royal Society of St. George a few years before. "England can take it" resounded around the world. British science and indomitable British courage came to help. Radar, then not yet betrayed by French turncoats to their German bosses, and rockets, another German

153

"invention" of latter days, helped the young heroes from the R. A. F., outnumbered though they were, and exposed to terrible losses, to beat back the air pirates.

At the end of August, 1940, the Prime Minister could give a long and comprehensive survey. France and the Lowlands had surrendered. England had been tried as no nation before. "Europe had a disastrous few months," Mr. Churchill said gravely. "So much so that at the beginning of May it would have seemed incredible that now we should actually be stronger than we had ever been before. It was essential to Hitler's prestige that he should continue his air attacks, as long," the seer added, "as any preoccupations he may have in respect to the Russian Air Force allow him to do so." Turning to the R. A. F. crews, he coined the historic phrase: "Never in the field of human conflict was so much owed by so many to so few."

The British Empire stood alone to save civilization. But Churchill's instinct, or perhaps his heritage in blood from Lady Randolph, told him that it would not always be so. "We hope our friends across the water will send us timely reenforcement."

Mr. Kennedy, then U. S. Ambassador to the Court of St. James's, grinned broadly from the Distinguished Visitors' Gallery. Subsequently he resigned to become a chief promoter of isolationism in United States.

Mr. Punch, it appears, understood the trend of the time better. He displayed Mr. Churchill in a new hat, singing an old song.

The Nazis satirize Churchill's eulogy of Neville Chamberlain

IN his eulogy of Neville Chamberlain, who passed away on November 9, 1940, Churchill paid his old antagonist high tribute: "I had the singular experience of passing in a day from being one of his most prominent opponents and critics to becoming one of his principal lieutenants, and on another day of passing from serving under him to become head of a government of which, with perfect loyalty, he was content to be a member. . . . Thereafter he acted with that singleness of purpose and simplicity of conduct, which at all times ought to be the ideal of us all. When he returned to duty a few weeks after a most severe operation, the bombardment of London and of the seat of government had begun. I was a witness during that fortnight, and I can testify that, although physically only the wreck of a man, his nerve was unshaken and his remarkable mental faculties unimpaired."

The King and his Prime Minister (*British Official Photo*)

ON November 14, 1940, Coventry was blitzed in an all-night air raid that killed 250 people and injured 800. The heroes of the R. A. F. retaliated on the same night with the first mass raid on Berlin. The House listened with deep emotion to the report given by the honorable and gallant Member for North St. Pancras, Squadron-Leader Grant-Ferris, who, a few hours before, had returned from the flaming skies over Berlin.

While the House was in session, the pirates were over London. They chose strategic targets. Seven hospitals and five convents were hit. At this very moment, Mr. Molotov took his train back to Moscow. The Zoo-Station, Berlin, was covered with Swastikas and Soviet Stars. Mr. Molotov's right breast-pocket bulged with the draft of a Neutrality and Friendship Agreement, soon to be known as the Moscow Pact. On November 20 the King opened a new session of Parliament. In his address from the Throne, he said: "I am confident that victory is assured."

From then on, both the King and Mr. Churchill devoted every free moment to visits in damaged areas and blitzed towns.

The Prime Minister on the Home Front's front line (*British Official Photo*)

IN the midst of a continuous air-raid warning, the Prime Minister visited Dover and Ramsgate, the front line in the battle for Britain. He inspected air-raid damage, and talked with local A. R. P. workers. He watched an air battle in which two Messerschmitts were shot down into the sea, right in front of him. Mostly for educational reasons, he temporarily replaced his famous John Bull hat with a steel helmet.

157

"It may be that in a few months' time people wearing shabby hats will be regarded as very patriotic." Sir Kingsley Wood
(*Punch*)

EVEN during the blitz the stories about Winston's funny headgear did not cease. Churchill's popularity had increased tremendously. The people loved him, and since they are English people they prefer to express their emotions by teasing.

The late Chancellor of the Exchequer defended his friend with a premonition which Mr. Punch preserved for days to come.

Prime Minister: "Are you managing to get plenty of food?" Dock worker: "Aye, aye, sir, we are doing grand, thank you!"

(*British Official Photo*)

ON one of his tours through battered docks the Prime Minister saw two dockers eating their meal. It belongs to those achievements on the home front of which Mr. Churchill is most proud, that rigidly rationed food is not distributed according to purchasing power, but according to the intensity of manual work. Hence the "British Restaurants," the factory canteens, serve a much heartier meal — for about an American quarter — than the Dorchester can offer its guests. The whole British population is much more healthily fed than in pre-war times, and Labor never had so balanced a diet.

Inspecting armored divisions (*British Official Photo*)

AN inspection of armored divisions took him through the North and the Midlands. Compared with American distances this is not a very long journey. But standing in a scout car (jeep) all the time? Passing tanks, guns, all sorts of vehicles in unending rows? Ever alert, ever smiling, ever the soldiers' father? And all that without the cigar? Isn't it a proof of fitness?

The Lady of No. 10 who, in her own words, spends her life "managing" her husband. (Copyright by Dorothy Wilding, London)

Old man Winston, fortified with cigar and well-
protected against bitter winter cold, watches a
demonstration of anti-aircraft gunnery.

(British Official Photo)

Accompanied by his man Friday, Sir Archibald Sinclair, Secretary of Air, the Prime Minister tensely watches flying display by new types of aircraft in southern England. This was one of the crucial moments for the further development of Britain's air power.

(British Official Photo)

Just the tiniest bit embarrassed, sixteen-year-old Georgie Smith, the youngest in the dockyards of Southampton, shakes hands with Mr. Churchill himself—a moment the lad will never forget. *(British Official Photo)*

163

Accompanied by his Excellency, Rauf Orbay, Turkish Ambassador, the Prime Minister inspects troops in the Southern Command. The pipe band of the Royal Scots was lined up in one of those English village streets. *(British Official Photo)*

The Churchills visit Polish troops in Scotland. At right, the late
General Sikorski.   (*British Official Photo*)

FLANKED by two fighting allies, the late General Sikorski commanding
the Polish Army, his country's war hero number one, as well as by his
wife, the Prime Minister visited Polish troops in Scotland, where winters
are cold. Mr. Churchill, it appears, pressed his lips tightly together. Perhaps he shivered a little in the Englishman's traditional mackintosh. Polish
chivalry would not let a beautiful lady freeze. Mrs. Churchill donned a
Polish gray coat.

The Prime Minister's official de luxe train has gone to war, and like all British subjects, Mr. Churchill subjects himself ungrudgingly to the tyranny of rigidly curtailed timetables. Grateful for a few minutes of reading time, Mr. Churchill waits for the train. (*British Official Photo*)

CHURCHILLS ALL (*Punch*)

THE year 1940 ended with a slight improvement on the credit side of the British ledger. Among the setbacks were the adherence of Hungary to the Fascist Tri-Party-Pact, De Valera's stubborn refusal to hand over the treaty ports to Britain, Laval's return to full puppet-power in France, after his farcical three-day prison term, and finally the announcement that in the month of November 4,588 civilians were killed and 6,202 injured in air raids on Britain. On the other hand, stubborn Greek resistance forced Badoglio's resignation from the command of the Italian campaign. Britain's Middle East Army, under General Wavell, assisted by the Royal Navy, the R. A. F., and Free French troops, suddenly launched an attack on the Italians in the Western Desert, and pierced Bardia's defenses. Above all, President Roosevelt introduced the Lend-Lease system that has since developed into Mutual Aid.

The proudest moment in Winston Churchill's private life, however, was this December day on which his son, Captain Randolph Churchill, bowed his way into the House, and delivered his maiden speech. It was not his own fault, the Captain insisted with a becoming smile, that he had not joined up earlier. He had tried and tried again. But perhaps the voters, in rejecting him, had feared "certain paternalistic influences." Forty years before young Winston himself had, in his own maiden speech, referred to "a certain splendid memory." Winston père listened anxiously, and with relish. Perhaps, who knows, "Grandolph," too, was listening — from somewhere in heavenly England.

Mr. Churchill buys a Flag for Russia from his wife. (*British Official Photo*)

ON June 22, 1941, Hitler attacked Russia along a front of 1,500 miles. The British Empire no longer stood alone in its epic fight for divine right and human freedom.

Although their own living standards were already near subsistence level, the people of Britain immediately collected funds to help the people of Russia in what was now to become, in turn the new allies' "finest hour." Mrs. Churchill headed the drive of the "Red Cross for Russia." Mr. Churchill was her first customer. Standing outside No. 10, he exchanged a banknote for the Red Cross emblem.

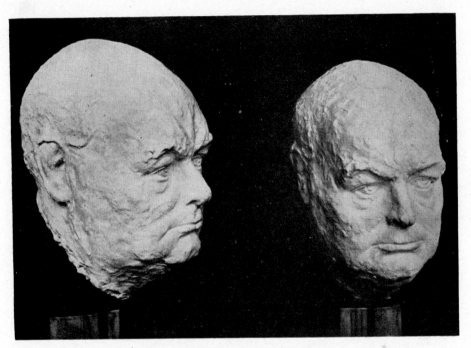

Two sculptures of Churchill by a Dutch artist in Sumatra who had
never seen him.   (*British Official Photo*)

THE air battle of Britain was won, but heavy German raiding subsisted.
The English Government was forced to call up every man and woman
between sixteen and sixty for compulsory A. R. P. work. In addition, Mr.
Bevin announced plans for general industrial conscription. Throughout
the first half of the year the danger of invasion of the British Isles was
breath-near. Winston Churchill's shadow loomed ever larger over the
globe.

A Dutch artist in Sumatra, who had never in his life seen the Prime
Minister, made, simply of plaster of Paris, two magnificent busts of
Churchill. Such was the British warlord's world-wide spell.

169

Goebbels' idea of Churchill
(*Kladderadatsch*)

Kladderadatsch, Berlin

IN a queer manner even Germany fell under this spell. The Nazis were drunk with victory. More and more vassals jumped upon Hitler's bandwagon. Rumania opened her country as a base for German troops. King Boris sold out Bulgaria, lest his family lose the immense estates owned by the Coburgs in Germany, Austria, and Czechoslovakia. The Fascists suffered reverses. South African and British colonial troops conquered Italian Somaliland. Mussolini admitted in a speech that Italy had already lost a fifth of her air force and a tenth of her army. Nevertheless, even if the Italian hyena was bleeding white, the Swastika was waving practically over the continent. Only England stood like a rock.

England? Or was it Churchill? Hitler believes in the superman. He was chilled to the marrow when the ghost of Churchill appeared in his sleepless nights. He tried to work off his inferiority complex in his habitual manner. "I herewith announce to the drunkard in Dophnig Street," (*Dophnig* Street is Hitler's pronunciation) he raged at Munich, "that Britain is threatened by a naval warfare such as you, Churchill, have never dreamed of."

A new propaganda barrage against the one invincible foe was let loose. Strangely, it did not work. The German masses hated as told. But single Germans, unorganized groups, began to ask themselves why the master race was not blessed with a Churchill.

Goebbels, with his sixth sense for the volatility of the crowd, stepped in. Vile and foul slander of the British Premier was radically stopped. It could work both ways. Certainly, Churchill was the archfoe. But was he superman? In this world there was space only for one superman. And for one superbrain.

170

Goebbels summoned all the outstanding cartoonists of Nazidom. "I wish a cartoon of Churchill," he decreed, "which shows his typical English pharisaism, his hypocrisy, his shopkeeper's shrewdness, but that neither distorts him nor lets him appear bigger than that drunkard really is."

Goebbels' order was punctiliously carried out. Mr. Churchill's suit is English tailor-made. His baldness is not exaggerated. The cigar is the genuine article. The expression of the face is repulsive, but more smart than menacing.

Kladderadatsch, as ever a specialist in German obscenity, was assigned to bring out the cartoon as frontispiece. The issue sold a million copies, four times the regular circulation, and subsequently hung in a million lavatories in respectable German homes. When the Gestapo made their habitual rounds, the first visit was to the W. C. (another Nazi nickname for Winston Churchill). If the picture was in good order, that is, covered with lascivious words and inscriptions, the family was all right.

Gradually the inscriptions faded. A lot of bombed-out Germans are saving the picture among their few precious possessions. To the inarticulate, unorganized Germans, hounded by the Himmler's spies, Churchill's cartoon has altered its meaning.

Winston's lion (Queen-Crowell Publishing Co.)

ANOTHER instance of Churchill's long-distance spell is the lion Rota. In August Churchill remarked with a touch of melancholy that his days of lion hunting were over. Like every tidbit of his off-the-record conversation, the *mot* went through the entire British press. Mr. George Thomson, a hunting gentleman in Kenya, read the lines. A few months later Rota arrived at Victoria Station, accompanied by her owner and two keepers. She was addressed to No. 10, but landed in the London Zoo, where she is at present the star attraction. Mr. Churchill promised to return the fur of the British Empire's symbol after its death to her rightful owner.

President meets the Prime
Minister at Atlantic Char-
ter Conference.
(*British Official Photo*)

ON August 14, 1941, the Atlantic Charter was released: the eight-point
issue of the meeting in Canadian waters between the President and the
Prime Minister. The text of the document was somewhat vague. It did not
contain any plan dealing with concrete questions. It rather expressed the
humanitarian aims of the two countries, and promised after the final
destruction of Nazi tyranny and disarmament of the aggressors, to work
for peace that would "ensure that all men may live out their lives in freedom from want and fear." The real practical result of the Atlantic Conference was that it initiated a long series of personal meetings between
the leaders of Hitler's opponents.

Churchill in Iceland (*British Official Photo*)

RETURNING to Britain, Mr. Churchill made a short stop in Iceland. Welcomed by Hermann Jonassen, Prime Minister of the country, Mr. Churchill emphasized his friendship for one of the oldest democracies in the world.

A salute in Rejkjavik harbor (*British Official Photo*)

HE returned aboard H.M.S. *Prince of Wales*. The crews of the freighters and whalers in Rejkjavik harbor gave him a rousing cheer. Mr. Churchill thanked them with his inimitable "V" salute.

United States War Department presents a globe to Mr. Churchill.
(*British Official Photo*)

THE fiendish attack on Pearl Harbor, on December 7, 1941, coincided — a fact that, strangely, is almost unknown in United States — with an attack on British territory in Malaya, and with Japanese air raids on Singapore and Hongkong. Now the *global* war was on.

As a fitting symbol, the U. S. War Department produced two enormous globes, each eighty inches in diameter and weighing, with its base, nearly half a ton. One globe was shipped to Mr. Churchill, the other presented to Mr. Roosevelt.

Subaltern Mary Churchill sees her father off on a trip to America.
(*British Official Photo*)

THE theoretical plans, expressed in the Atlantic Charter, no longer met the situation. A new personal meeting between President and Prime Minister became necessary. Aboard H.M.S. *Duke of York*, Mr. Churchill again crossed the ocean. With a smiling display of strict military discipline, his daughter, Subaltern Mary Churchill, saw her father off.

En route to America, May, 1943 (*British Official Photo*)

DURING his voyage Mr. Churchill spent most of his time dealing with official papers and news reports from London, and in discussions with the ministers and senior officers accompanying him. He took his meals in his cabin. Sometimes he mounted the bridge, or took a turn on the deck.

Churchill about to go ashore on arriving in America. First stop Washington, then to Quebec for another historic conference.
(*British Official Photo*)

The men who got the Prime Minister to the conference and back line up to have a last look at their admired passenger, as he was leaving.
(*British Official Photo*)

Churchill displays his siren suit in Washington (*British Official Photo*)

MR. CHURCHILL thrilled the White House by displaying his "siren suit." It is a one-piece garment with zip fastener which can be donned in a minute. The First Lady was so strongly impressed that she told her press conference she would have a similar garment made for her own husband.

On his special train Churchill reads dispatches with Mrs. Churchill
beside him.   (*British Official Photo*)

FOR his journeys throughout Canada and the United States, the Prime
Minister used a special car as a time-saving measure — to work with his
secretaries while traveling.

Churchill at Ottawa, December 30, 1941 (*British Official Photo*)

MR. CHURCHILL spent Christmas Eve in the White House — "far from my country, far from my family, yet I cannot truthfully say that I feel far from home." On December 26 he addressed both the U. S. Senate and the House of Representatives in joint session. Three days later he crossed the border into Canada. On December 30 he spoke to the Canadian law-makers. The tenor of this memorable speech was: "Preparation . . . liberation . . . assault." Enthusiastic crowds had gathered in front of Parliament Building. Mr. Churchill received their cheers with open arms, as if he wanted to press to his heart all Canada.

With his massive figure framed in the doorway of the Canadian Parliament Buildings, East Block, Mr. Churchill enters to attend a special meeting of the Canadian Cabinet's War Committee

(British Official Photo)

Churchill inspecting Canadian Naval Cadets at Ottawa (*British Official Photo*)

LATER, with the impressive Canadian Government House as a perfect background, the Prime Minister inspected cadets of the rapidly developing Royal Canadian Navy. And so to Quebec, to the Victory Conference.

Churchill arrives in Quebec (*British Official Photo*)

MR. CHURCHILL arrived in the conference city almost unnoticed. He walked between Mrs. Churchill and his old friend and colleague Mr. King, the Canadian Premier. Only a small crowd of casual onlookers happened to see the distinguished guest. Mr. Churchill greeted them with an affable smile.

Churchill leaving a joint session of the Anglo-Canadian War Cabinets in Quebec. MacKenzie King, Prime Minister of Canada, is at his right. The conferees are visibly satisfied with their discussion. They had resolved to conquer North Africa. (*British Official Photo*)

MacKenzie King, President Roosevelt, and Mr. Churchill on the terrace of the Citadel overlooking Quebec (*British Official Photo*)

On his return from Canada, Mr. Churchill and his daughter Mary
spent two hours at Niagara. Here, at Thompson's Point, they are admir-
ing the view of the whirlpool. (*British Official Photo*)

Entraining for Washington, Mr. Churchill obliges a little girl who begged him for a cigar band from one of his famous weeds.

(British Official Photo)

The Prime Minister walks with his duffle-coated daughter and Mrs. Churchill on the deck of H.M.S. Renown, the battleship which brought them home. (British Official Photo)

Churchill in Moscow, August, 1942, as seen in U.S.S.R. Newsreel
(*British Official Photo*)

IN August, 1942, the indefatigable wanderer made his least advertised, but probably most momentous, state visit. The Russians had already advanced far in their magnificent comeback against the invader. All Britain thrilled at Stalin's success. The Prime Minister was anxious for a personal meeting. Mr. Stalin warmly welcomed the suggestion, and invited Mr. Churchill.

The U. S. S. R. newsreels showed a strange, unkempt, tight-lipped, pugnacious, old Churchill.

West and East smile at each other for the first time.
(*British Official Photo*)

Ismet Inonu, President of Turkey, smiles as he receives Mr. Churchill on the Prime Minister's first stop between Moscow and Cairo. Turkish military experts and statesmen joined in the conversation.

(*British Official Photo*)

190

In Cairo, Mr. Churchill stayed at the British Embassy. Here he sits in the Embassy garden, wearing his famed siren suit and a "ten-gallon" hat ideally suited for protection against Cairo's August heat.

(*British Official Photo*)

At Cyprus, the Acting Greek Archbishop guided Mr. Churchill around the island. (*British Official Photo*)

General Jan Christian Smuts, who kept a rendezvous in Cairo with Mr. Churchill, plays with Master Victor Lampson, the Ambassador's little son. *(British Official Photo)*

Major Randolph's own progeny, Winston Churchill, Jr., is temporarily fatherless, even at Christmas. Here Mrs. Alexander, wife of the present First Lord, plays Santa to him at the Admiralty Building
(British Official Photo)

Major Randolph Churchill, the Prime Minister's son, is an officer in the Allied Combined Operations Service, which combines intelligence and liaison work with actual combat. This picture was taken somewhere in Tunisia. (*British Official Photo*)

The supreme war lord, all alone, gazes at the El Alamein position.
(*British Official Photo*)

The Prime Minister wanted to see his Middle East Forces in action. Here, at an advanced outpost of the 8th Army, he is flanked by Generals Alexander (left) and Montgomery (right)
(*British Official Photo*)

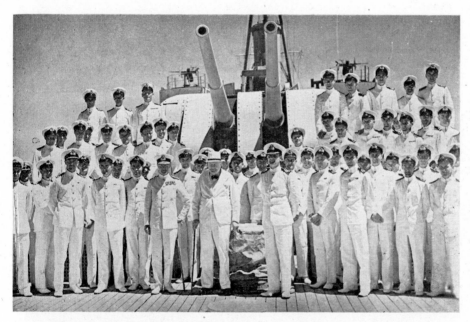

Men of a submarine depot ship in a North African port pose with
Mr. Churchill.   (*British Official Photo*)

UNDER a burning sun, and under climatic conditions which might have
deterred another man, Mr. Churchill visited a submarine depot ship in a
North African port. He thanked the men for their wonderful contribution
to the war. He inspected the Guard of Honor, mingled with the crews,
shook hands with each submarine commander, and addressed the ship's
company. His visit had to be restricted to one hour. Officers and men
wanted to keep a souvenir of this stirring hour, and were photographed
with their visitor.

At the end of his desert tour, the Prime Minister bids farewell to the ground crews of an airfield. His departure is scarcely ceremonial.

(*British Official Photo*)

Churchill thanks the Merchant Navy. (*British Official Photo*)

THE English people breathed easier when peripatetic old Winston had returned safely. Bluejackets and dockworkers surrounded the homecomer, and asked him to say something. Mr. Churchill had no news from Africa. But he proved amazingly informed about the life, the labor, the hard struggle, and the great contribution to the war effort the tars and dockers were making. When Churchill ended, the motley crowd was too spellbound to cheer.

Churchill and General Smuts inspect defense installations in
Southeast England. (*British Official Photo*)

IN the autumn of 1942, improvement in arms and defenses claimed much
of the Prime Minister's time and attention. Moreover, veteran General
Smuts, Mr. Churchill's guest in October, had to be fittingly entertained.

A highly respectable family watch is a battle-drill demonstration by British Infantry.   (*British Official Photo*)

Mr. Churchill, the expert, examines closely the new rifle and short bayonet, latest equipment of the Unit. General Ismay is at extreme left, and General Sir Bernard Paget is at right.   (*British Official Photo*)

The greatest man in our time, and the cleverest woman.
(*British Official Photo*)

Another Casablanca friendship: General Henri Giraud and General DeGaulle shake hands. (*British Official Photo*)

Mr. Churchill at the center of things: Real war leadership in action. Anthony Eden, Sir Alan Brooke, Air Chief Marshal Tedder, Admiral Sir Andrew Cunningham, General Marshall, America's top-soldier, General Eisenhower, and General Montgomery—all the Allied galaxy watch the Prime Minister's every movement. (*British Official Photo*)

The Sultan of Morocco visits the President at Casablanca, and Mr. Churchill sits in. The Prime Minister looks completely detached; he has long outgrown oriental glamour.

(*British Official Photo*)

A serious conversation with General Marshall and General Montgomery, the Allied fighting chiefs.   (*British Official Photo*)

Mr. Churchill, in his uniform of Air Commodore, RAF, receives his chiefs-of-staff at his Anfa villa. Lord Louis Mountbatten stands behind the Prime Minister.   (*British Official Photo*)

Lord Mountbatten, an old friend of Mr. Churchill's, emerges from a conference as Supreme Commander of Allied Armies in the Southeast Pacific. He may be fated to fire the last shot of the war.

(*British Official Photo*)

Churchill visits British troops at Tripoli (*British Official Photo*)

THE Prime Minister could not leave, nor did he want to, without having visited the British troops in Tripoli. The first regiment to enter Tripoli was the 11th Hussars. They had also been the spearhead capturing Tobruk and Benghazi during the 1,600-mile advance of the 8th Army from El Alamein. Mr. Churchill must meet them.

Mr. Churchill and General Montgomery at Tripoli (*British Official Photo*)

CASABLANCA was a success. President Roosevelt termed it the "unconditional surrender conference." The grand strategy against Japan was decided upon. The assault on Nazi Europe was firmly resolved. Seeing eye to eye, the British war lord and General Montgomery, commander of the British troops for the invasion, made their last public appearance in Africa.

Field Marshal Smuts with the Churchills in the garden at No. 10
Downing Street, October, 1943.   (*British Official Photo*)

IN October, 1943, Field-Marshal Smuts reappeared in England. He had
come at the invitation of the British Government "for consultation and
discussions," and he joined the Inner War Cabinet for the duration of his
visit. The *Oubaas* was a frequent guest in No. 10.

Two Cellars. "I thought that would warm you, sir: I am sorry not to be able to manage a little more coal as well." (*Punch*)

THE idyll, of course, was delusive. Two dangers menaced England. The coal output was decreasing, and the sinkings of Allied ships in the Atlantic were again on the upgrade. The coal output remained a headache. Mr. Churchill obtained lease of the Azores from Portugal, Britain's ally since the fourteenth century. The newly acquired naval and air base greatly reduced the U-boat menace throughout the Atlantic.

ALL TOGETHER. "Hold it! Another year or so and you've got 'em!"

(*Punch*)

Many a street of Valletta, Malta, the worst-blitzed town in the world, was still a shambles. Mr. Churchill preferred to walk alone. (*British Official Photo*)

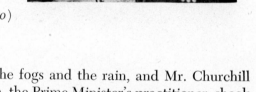

Mr. Churchill with Field Marshal Lord Gort at Malta. (*British Official Photo*)

AND so November came, and the fogs and the rain, and Mr. Churchill coughed a little, and Lord Moran, the Prime Minister's practitioner, shook his head, and said: "No!"

The Prime Minister could not, of course, explain, not even to his friend and doctor of long years' standing, why his journey was so urgent, indeed, more important for early victory than anything else, his own health included. Meekly, he pretended that he wanted to visit Malta. In fact, it was not at all a pretense. Mr. Churchill did visit the battered, glorious island. The people of Malta gave him an enthusiastic reception. Field Marshal Lord Gort piloted the Prime Minister through Valletta, the capital city.

The Allied leaders at Teheran (*British Official Photo*)

THE Old Man was in a hurry. He could not miss his rendezvous in Teheran with Roosevelt and with Stalin. It would be the first time that the President and the Marshal — indeed, that all three leaders of the United Nations would meet in person.

They got along well, if one may trust the lens. Mr. Churchill, looking more massive than ever in his Air Commodore's uniform, was backed by his daughter Sarah, as well as by Mr. Anthony Eden. The President was all smiles. Even Stalin unbent.

Mr. Churchill presents the Stalingrad Sword to Marshal Stalin at Teheran

(British Official Photo)

TOWARD the beginning of the Teheran Conference, Mr. Churchill presented the Stalingrad Sword to Marshal Stalin. It was a solemn ceremony. All the prominent members of both missions were present in the Soviet Legation. Both the British and the Soviet national anthems were played. The sword which the Prime Minister handed over to the Marshal was the gift of King George to Stalingrad.

The Shah of Persia greets Mr. Churchill at Teheran on the Prime
Minister's sixty-ninth birthday.　　　　　(*British Official Photo*)

THE climax of Teheran was a non-political event: Mr. Churchill's sixty-
ninth birthday. The young Shah of Persia arrived to render homage to
Britain's war lord. The Oriental sovereign saluted in the most rigid military
manner.

Officers of the Shah of Persia's bodyguard line up at Teheran to offer
their congratulations. (*British Official Photo*)

Lance Corporal Sutcliffe presents the Prime Minister with a gift on behalf of the Forces of Persia and Iraq.
(*British Official Photo*)

With a subtle touch of humor, the British Press Unit presents a caracul hat to their senior colleague.
(*British Official Photo*)

Mr. Churchill and cake with sixty-nine candles (*British Official Photo*)

HE seemed a little more thoughtful while looking at the birthday cake the two big allies had contributed to the dinner party Mr. Churchill gave. Sixty-nine candles . . .

217

Marshal Stalin gives Mr. Churchill a birthday toast (*British Official Photo*)

BUT he regained his most engaging and, as it were, slightly embarrassed smile, when Stalin after dinner toasted the United Nations, "at this particularly fitting day, Mr. Churchill's birthday."

Marshal and Prime Minister take leave with firm handshake
(*British Official Photo*)

Mr. Churchill recovering from his illness in December, 1943.

(*Sphere*-Crown Copyright)

ON December 16, the House of Commons was startled, and the whole Empire perturbed, by Vice-Premier Attlee's disclosure that Mr. Churchill had another attack of the same illness that already had befallen him after his departure from Casablanca, in February, 1943. Then the attack had been played down. It had been pneumonia, but it had lasted only ten days, during which Mr. Churchill carried on his work incessantly.

This time the attack was worse. Mr. Churchill had already a slight rise in temperature when he left for the Middle East on November 1. He insisted that it was only the result of inoculations and of a cold and a slight laryngitis. His daughter Sarah and his son Randolph assisted Lord Moran and two service doctors in tending the unruly patient.

But after the strenuous, elaborate celebration of Mr. Churchill's birthday in Teheran there was little doubt left that pneumonia was back. Not quite two weeks after the recurring attack the Prime Minister issued a personal statement, declaring that "a few weeks in sunshine are necessary to restore my physical strength" and that he was proceeding to an undisclosed destination to recuperate. It was rumored, but never confirmed, that Mr. Churchill recuperated by writing a film scenario about the life of Marlborough.

Mrs. Churchill had joined her husband as soon as the first news of his illness came. She "managed" him so successfully that the doctors soon allowed their patient to spend a little time out of doors in the sunshine.

Fit again, the Prime Minister returns to London, January, 1944

IN another personal statement Mr. Churchill revealed that not at any time had he had to relinquish his part in the direction of affairs, and now felt able to transact his business fully.

He returned to London toward the end of January, 1944, completely restored in health, in his favorite Elder Brother of Trinity uniform, and with a happy smile at his companion.

Mr. Churchill displays his uniforms: Left to right, as Colonel of the Fourth Hussars, in nautical kit, in his caracul cap, in tropical white, and as Air Commodore.

TAKING BACK THE REINS. "Plenty of luggage, I see, as usual." (*Punch*)

THERE is no end to Churchill's work and duties. The old English stage-coach will be heavily loaded with post-war problems. But the coachman holds the reins in two skillful, firm hands. Winston drives on.

LOOKING BETTER (*Punch*)

THE round earth is still badly beaten and bruised. But Dr. Churchill notices an improvement. Just look into the rising sun. Everything looks better. The end of the war is near. 1944?

Illustrations

Illustrations

Illustrations

Illustrations

Illustrations

Illustrations

231

Illustrations

232